KAREN
STANSON

GOODCHILD

A KINK OF A LIFE

Paul Goodchild

Jun 2006.

THE STRANBERRY

FAIRPLAYSTERS

PENNINE PENS
2005

Published 2006 by Pennine Pens
Copyright © the author
All rights reserved

ISBN: 1 873378 62 9

Published by Pennine Pens.
32, Windsor Road, Hebden Bridge,
West Yorkshire, HX7 8LF.
Tel 01422-843724
books@penninepens.co.uk
www.hebdenbridge.co.uk
www.penninepens.co.uk

About Paul Goodchild

Born in 1947 Paul Goodchild experienced the joys and vicissitudes of growing up in 1950s Britain. After coming of age during the cultural revolution of the 1960s he was inspired/distracted into pursuing a variety of false idols and truthful byways. Lucky enough to meet an understanding soul-mate, he is the father of two children (25 and 23) and managed to survive the the Thatcher years living a low-budget creative lifestyle without paying much tax.

Now a fully reformed character, he has for the last ten years been a sometime schoolteacher/ researcher and festival funster, and participant in New Labour's Socialist utopia.

His remaining ambition is to inspire the opening of a network of radical residential Real-Life Skills Colleges for young people in the 14-17 age group based on the model of Denmark's Efterskoles.

Previous Publications

Two-Tone Home 1978 (poetry)

Adam Turner Adventures
Blue Angel Quest 1996
The Sword of Justice 2000

In Progress

The Gold Mace Black Race an Adam Turner Adventure
The Khacik of Kharabanda A fantasy
A Kink of a Life: the second half of a story of our times: 1976-2006.

Introduction

Why *A Kink of a Life?* Personally I'm a fairly straight and narrow person but my life has been full of so many uninvited kinks that I have adapted and made a habit of it. I've never had a job for more than 6 months and that only twice. I've survived on the margins for the last thirty years without being dishonest apart from bending a few rules and regulations.

I saw the Coronation twice, nearly ran over a fox outside Buckingham Palace at the moment Princess Di died in Paris, had a dysfunctional childhood with death, incest and thirteen schools, was a revolting student in London and Paris 1968, had a Kalashnikov stuck in my face in Arabia in 1974, passed through Iran just before Khomeini, Afghanistan just before the Russians, got chased up a lamp post by the crowds in New Delhi on India's 40th anniversary of Independence Day, mingled with celebrities, met Blair, Benn, Blunkett and Straw (fat lot of good that did me!), shook hands with Chuck Berry, smoked dope with Howard Marks, drunk milk from the same cow as the Dalai Lama, visited twenty Danish Free schools, taught in twenty English ones, re-built a ruin up a Spanish mountain, married and had two children, drove to Sri Lanka, hitch-hiked to Ethiopia and saw the world's first jumbo jet crash and Concorde land for the last time

More importantly, due to the combination of these uninvited, thought-provoking changes and the use of mind-expanding drugs and thanks to the visionaries and hard-working tax payers of once-Great Britain's 'Welfare State' I acquired a personal and political consciousness that has enabled and ennobled my sometimes blundering path through life.

My aim with this book is to share some of the sights and insights of coming of age during 50 of the most interesting years in human history.

Paul Goodchild, *Atalbeiter Granada.*

Welfare State Baby

25th November 1947

I was born in a kink of history at the heart and end of Empire in St George's Hospital, Hyde Park Corner, London, overlooking King George's back yard and spent the first five years of my life living underneath the pavement in Victoria.

My Dad was a cook in the hospital. He bought my Mum kippers for breakfast, which might explain my Charlie Chaplin feet. Born as a grass is always greener Sagittarian and in a period of post-war euphoria gave me a boundless sense of optimism that has carried me through the happiness-crinkling experiences of my kink of a life. Being a big-boned, powdered milk-munching beneficiary of the brand new Welfare State helped. Years later I would bungle and bluff my way into brand new concrete-and-glass Essex University and learn nothing for the cost of nothing – except how to think. A funny aside is me arriving at the Labour Party Conference of 1995 with my new Youth School plan. Walking into a hall, Tony Blair was on the telly saying 'Education, Education, Education'. In a back room David 'Comrade' Triesman, one-time Lenin lookalike with hair, the man with the red Cortina who would never give lifts at University, was introducing the notion that it was about time free student grants and fees were abolished, like Lenin, he became general secretary to the Party but I don't expect he'll be dying for his beliefs.

Anyway, back to the story. The ensuing years were mostly a blank. I never remembered my real Dad even when I first met him aged 11; more on the reasons why later. There were sisters who disappeared and were replaced with little brothers. A huge grandmother with a sunbeam smile, pictures of an ecstatic child being pushed in pram by big-busted sister in Hyde Park or sat on a see-saw with two glum siblings.

Memories of queuing for rations, London's last tram-lines, tonsils out opposite the jellied eel shop in Victoria, window gazing with Gran in the giant Army and Navy Stores, walking into a lamp-post aged 3 conveniently placed outside a hospital, sulphurous pea-soup fogs from a million coal fires, playing on bombsites left by the Blitz and one day caught singing carols as I peed in the drain when my Mum came out to give the singers a penny.

Later, later, later, through several layers of life I was sitting in a study room at Essex University tripping on LSD when this big knot in my brain suddenly relaxed and I remembered my first conscious thought "Oh, no not this again ..."

I awoke to a beery, leery looking stepfather shaking my cot. I knew I would have to watch out because here was a character not quite in control of himself. Only sudden death would eventually separate us

I still can't really decide whether I was used to being rudely awoken and it finally registered as a thought, or as a new human being with just-formed consciousness, I was awakening to another futile incarnation that I would have to work my way through en route to Nirvana.

DARDANELLES AND DUNKERQUE

HOW WINSTON CHURCHILL NEARLY KILLED MY GRANDAD AND DAD AND ENDED UP EDUCATING ME!

Bishop Grundvigt, the brains behind the Danish free School movement set great store by the study of history and folklore. If we don't know where we come from then how do we know where we are going? In a society dominated by change, the itinerant pursuit of work and the breakdown of the nuclear family it's hard finding your roots, not least due to one's own need to change, adapt, earn a living and put down your own roots in a fast-changing world.

I've been lucky enough to unravel some of my own family history and it turns out that I'm thrice lucky to be alive – a lot of bullets and bombs went whizzing by my forbears, all with someone else's name on them.

The best picture I have of my maternal Grandad Willy Barrat was in a blacksmith's shop in South Africa during the Boer War grinning his head off flanked by a couple of cheerful Zulus. In 1914 he re-enlisted to fight the Germans, the Turks and whoever else needed sorting out. In 1915 Winston Churchill had the bright idea of creeping up on the Turks via the Dardanelles and knocking them out of the war. It was a good plan, except Kemal Ataturk, their best general, (later to become President and founding father of modern Turkey) was in charge and knew the British and Australians were coming. I sometimes wonder if the job of politicians of the right is to acknowledge that there are too many people on the planet and then dream up fiendish schemes for slimming the population down – it's still happening today in Iraq – and anyway, war is always good for business, producing new technology and usually prolonging the shelf-life of those that start it. But the innocent always pay.

Somebody once said to me: "Of course it was you lot in the 1970s with your free love that started the one-parent family craze." Bollocks! How many fit spunky men have killed each other in the major and minor wars that happened last century? It's a good job the women-folk were left to pick up the pieces. They had three generations of one-parent experience by the time it came to the 1970s.

My Mum's attitude to the Welfare State was, "Get what you can off them. My Dad fought in the Boer war for those bastards".

In the Dardenelles caper the Royal Navy could not get in close enough to land the British Troops so Grandad Barrat got stuck in a wooden boat with 30 men to land on the shore of Asia Minor and make war. The locals had dug themselves in with machine gun pits and rifle trenches. Just to be sure the enemy were sitting ducks they strung barbed wire on the beach and underneath the water. The men in the boats didn't stand a chance. The water turned red with their blood. Willy Barratt lived to tell the tale only because he landed behind a boulder and stayed there while his mates, tangled in barbed wire beneath the water, were cut to pieces.

He survived the Great War and went home with a smile on his face and made my Mum. However, like so many of his generation he was never quite right in his health afterwards. Luckily for him Fanny Louise Swift, his missus, was as tall, bold and big-hearted as her husband. He worked in the first Ford plant and she started a lodging house in Manchester. Next there was a corner shop selling Woodbines and her homemade pies. My Mum got her boxer's broken nose as a kid while standing in the cellar watching the men unloading boxes of pop bottles down a chute until one of them collided with her face.

Soon there was a small pub in mid Wales, then another and finally a pukka Hotel, The Red Lion in Llanamanarch with its front in England and the back in Wales. It was where the local hunt met and the taffs would go round the front for a pint on their teetotal Sundays. Grandad was retired due to ill-health by then and had his own bar in the back where he would generously drink his way through the fruits of his wife's labour. Still, Fanny Barratt knew how to share it around and she would send milk and bread with my Mum to the poor of the village. One of Mum's memories was of the drunken pig.

This pig used to be given the slops from drawing off the keg beer. He developed such a taste for it that one day he got in the cellar door, boozed all the drainings from the barrels and then ran around the yard and bit off all the chickens' heads.

My Mum, despite her broken nose was turning into a blonde beauty. A lot of the lads in the county were hunting after her including the heir to the Valspar paint family. She was to have a big 16th 'coming out' party at the hotel. Unfortunately Willy Barratt died one week before and it was cancelled. On top of that Granny Barratt had to give up the hotel – in the 1930s British women could not hold a licence. Everything that she had worked for and built up from her first house in Manchester was thus lost and the old coaching inn, the Red Lion, was sold off cheap in the depressed economic climate of the 1930s. **

She stayed on long enough to wind things up and enjoy the attentions of an old admirer from London (I wonder what those lucky ladies got up to in the War?) Frank Fletcher was his name (nice bit of rhyming slang in there somewhere) and he got this lad Peter Goodchild to chauffeur him up in his boss's sports car – he was only seventeen. Him and Lottie hit it off straight away and he once told me tales of taking her out chasing rabbits by headlight – that must have been how sister Dorrie got made.

Peter was back off to London blissfully oblivious until my Mum turned up three months later with a bunny in the oven. Peter was a single-parent child too. His Mum was a dancer and his Dad owned the first cinema in Shoreham, near Brighton. It could have been a good business but it didn't last that long because Grandad Goodchild died 30 years too young on account of the mustard gas poisoning he got in the First World War.

Granny Goodchild couldn't handle three growing boys on her own and they ended up in a Catholic quasi-orphanage in West Grinstead, Sussex, just as I would end up in a similar situation 30 years later (as the captain of Churchill House!). It was run first by the Sisters of Mercy and then the Christian Brothers. Here the blue-eyed twins would encounter the sexual abuse that they would pass on to their own children. (More on this later, see Flyaway Peter, Flyaway Paul, in book 2)

The first home Peter and Lottie shared was in Paddington but they were over half way through the 1930s and the Depression had hit London's 'good life' that they lived on and served: her catering and him driving. They moved to live with Mum's stepsister Lilly and Uncle George in Runcorn, Cheshire. He was a timekeeper at I.C.I., one of the economic jewels in the crown of the empire. He got Peter a steady job there. The freewheeling lad-about-town from London's West End must have hated it, living in Coronation Street style terraced back to backs with the company timekeeper!

Saved by the gong of war, he went to work one day and didn't come back for 6 years. He went to London and enlisted without telling my Mum until after the event. Arriving at the enlisting station the sergeant told him to go home. My Dad, understandably, was insistent.

"No, no. Go away, son."

"I'm not going anywhere. I've come from up North to enlist."

"Listen, son, stop bothering me or I'll have you arrested." Purple-faced my old man furiously insisted on enlisting.

"Look, you enlisted this morning, so go away, you can't enlist twice!" By sheer coincidence he had enlisted at the same station as his twin brother Paul. Although in different units they ended up on the same beach at Dunkirk and eventually Dad was posted as my uncle's driver in Cyprus. Big war, small world.

Mum survived the war first by being sent to safe countryside Scotland where she caught rabbits to feed herself and Dorrie and then to London where, despite the bombing, she must have had an interesting time amongst those fleeting legions of men gathering for war.

My sister Jaqueline was conceived around this time. There was often mention of a Frenchman called Jacomet and my mother used to love practising her pidgin phrases of French with a cheeky grin on her face. Although my Dad had home leave and was Jackie's Dad. It came out that Jacomet was her father just before my Mum died. I never really digested this fact until I just wrote her name: Jaqueline – Jacomet!

My Dad, like Grandad Baratt before him, survived two beaches, the first was Dunkerque, where he ended up meeting both his two brothers, from different regiments. The second gave him a permanent blink caused by constant artillery bombardment, the beach head at Anzio in the invasion of Italy, another brilliant population-control manoeuvre by Churchill and his chums, with the loss of thousands of Allied lives, bless their souls.

He told me of a couple of his heroic deeds, managing to go through a war without killing anyone. The first was when he was on guard duty at night; big rustling in the bushes: "Halt! Who goes there?"

No reply. BANG! Silence. In the morning investigation a very undead cow munching in the field behind the hedge!

Outside of Tripoli, just after the British victory at El Alamein driving along the highway alone in an empty truck he sees a troop of dishevelled Germans trudging towards him.

"Oh, fuck!" says he. The Bedford trucks were 'armed' with a .303

rifle slung over the windscreen, pointing the wrong way. To use it, the driver would have to cock the bolt, stick the butt out of the window, change hands and then point it at the enemy. Some chance. The old man decided to blag it. He skidded to a halt and shouted out, "Right, you lot, what are you doing?" The Germans put up their hands and surrendered. Now he had to stick them in the truck and take them into the chaos of liberated Tripoli. Nobody wanted them, least of all the flustered Military Police.

Being an ex-private hire driver from London he knew his cities and he headed for the hospital; just the right place. His prisoners were medical orderlies. Lucky them. Lucky him. He survived the war and came home with a smile on his face. Mum had a nice pad and lots of connections and they settled into post-war bliss.

Churchill, the war specialist, got the push from the socialist working class camaraderie created by the war. The new Labour government laid the seeds of the Welfare State that would feed body, mind and soul of their love-child, conceived in early 1947. Thus I was born a wide-eyed peace baby, ready but unsteady for the new epoch!!

**Glastonbury Weekend 2004*

I pulled in at the Red Lion for a trip down memory lane, a classic Georgian coaching house. The three stone steps were outside where the ladies of the hunt my mother had told me about would mount side-saddle. Out the back a collection of broken-down stables and sheds were piled with a jumble of worthless ironmongery and three-legged tables. Inside an awful sixties attempt at conversion into an Elizabethan theme failed in a nasty mish-mash of stucco and stuck-on fake wood beams. An ageing landlord served from a decrepit bar and next door a bunch of surly local lads played tunes on an out-of-date juke box and eyed a suspicious policeman in a patrol car outside.

I ordered drinks and asked the old boy if he had ever heard of my grand-mother, Mrs Barratt.

"Oh, yes, I should do. I have been here forty years and was born the day your grandfather died, and was delivered by the midwife who certified him dead." It turned out his cousin Tommy Bowen had played with my uncle Peter. I went to visit him and he told of his playmate who had moved away when his dad died. In the death of these two grandfathers lay the roots of two generations of dysfunctional children.)

1950: Belgravia

Chocolate Ladies Trauma

Victoria 1950 was a busy place. Five years since the war and Britain was rebuilding with the help of the American Marshall plan that would change our culture and leave us in debt for 100 years. We were living under the pavement next to a corner newsagent's on the junction of Belgrave Road and Warwick Way.

People didn't steal or molest babies then so my Mum used to leave me on the pavement in my pram where she could keep an eye on me although it was a major crossroads about 300 yards behind Victoria Station.

My Dad was still around and they used to argue about my hair being kept long, a bushy blonde Afro of curls. I have no memories of cars, only an old man with a funny hat and a bicycle with strings of onions; a French onion-seller.

The only other thing I could remember were the backs of ladies' legs standing on the corner in high-heeled shoes. Further up from my baby gaze they had short skirts and leopard skin coats topped with peroxide blonde hair. Every so often one of them would go away and come back again. She would go straight into the corner shop, buy a chocolate bar and give it to the loverlee baybee!

I was the unrequited love-object of the ladies of the street circa 1950. My Mum would come to get me in at the end of the day and find a little chocolate-faced blonde Afro-babe. I've had a problem with chocolate and the ladies ever since. I've had teeth pulled in India and Egypt and my head turned by women all over the world until I've got a permanent pain in the neck.

The most dangerous job I ever had was as a motorcycle courier in London after returning from 6 months in Arabia and remote Kenya. I had to give up looking at women before I was killed. It was a double trauma that would remain with me for the rest of my life as if coming of age in the peace and love sixties and trying to maintain a marriage in single-parent Britain wasn't going to be hard enough anyway.

I'm not sure whether I've had more chocolate bars or bouts of sex but what I do know is that women have taught me most of what I know and I haven't got many teeth left!

1952: Twin Coronations

Imust have been about 4 when I saw the Coronation of Queen Elizabeth - twice. Life had gone foggy and my other memories of this time are dim on account of the breakdown of my parents' marriage. The funny thing about parental separation is that it divides the mind of the young child so that the mass of thoughts and memories are incomplete, one-sided, if you like. The reference points have moved so therefore everything becomes ill-defined.

My parents divorced after my father's seduction of my sister Dorrie and his imprisonment for four years in Wormwood Scrubs. I would have been about 2-3 years old and have no visual memory of my father at all. Shortly afterwards my mother went into hospital with pleurisy. I remember visiting with my sisters. Later, she'd often speak of Dr Ray at the Gordon Hospital. "I was his favourite patient, you know… " like it was a holiday or a honeymoon. She never did have a proper holiday in my memory.

There's also a recollection of my first sexual experience. Waking up in my cot in a strange house and taking all my clothes off. A lady with dark hair came and scolded me and made me put them back on again. There was a window that looked down on a street with no houses opposite, only trees. Along the way a big red slab of something was propped over the road. In the middle there was a big, white, circular sign with a line through it with writing on it. It was that 200 yds Look Left Look Right vista of a new young soul trying to make sense of their surroundings, but mine had changed from inner Belgravia to outer suburbia.

In a déja vu moment 13 years later on a Sunday afternoon leave out from boarding school in Wanstead E11. I would walk past the house and recognise it while trying to find the house of a girl I had met but didn't have the address of. Ahead of me a red bridge bearing the London Underground logo on it proclaimed Loughton Station. I had found a tiny part of my fractured roots.

I was living with strangers and at nursery school with strangers in that kind of unquestioning vacuum where everything is new to the eyes of a child. One day the teacher said, "We're going to London to see the Queen."

"Oh, good," I thought, imagining sooty giant buildings, massive shop windows, red soldiers marching in lines, cheering people, giants with plumed helmets and black horses that dropped untidy but interesting steaming mounds on the road. I didn't have any images or expectations of my lost family; mother, sister etc, but then, human beings particularly new ones are without malice and with their best face to the future often take for granted their spouses/mothers that provide the emotional and sometimes spiritual stability to their lives. Essentially, I suppose I was experiencing that on my ownness/distrust of emotional depth that I carry with me today despite being a husband father and "friends" with hundreds of others.

We were taken, not to a big sooty organic London but to a high street of pink new bricks and neat shops. We went into this big room, sat down as all the lights were turned off, leaving us in a velvety darkness for a split second. Suddenly on the wall golden coaches galloped by with booming music and thousands of people, some throwing flowers, with marching red soldiers and troops with ponytailed helmets riding black horses. I was watching the Coronation the second time around and I was in my first cinema show. It must have taken some months to produce the film for all the school kids in the country to see. I had seen the real thing and felt cheated. I wasn't going to London to see the Queen, or my Mum.

I've always found it difficult to take most films seriously and would never go to a cinema on my own.

1953: SURREY

ALL NEW – COUNCIL ESTATE KIDS

It was all new. There were rows of toy town houses backed by countryside. This was a world beyond London, green, treeful, hilly. Mum was there in a yellow dress. Denny the stepfather was digging pale red clods of earth in the garden. I'm not sure where I had come from. There is no connection in my mind between basementville Victoria and the New Town. I only remember arriving at the end of a very long black tunnel into what was my first experience of countryside. Maybe I had been in care, or my Gran had brought me down. Where we had arrived was Merstraham, Surrey, on the London-Brighton line, an example of the Labour Party's post-war building programme with semi-detached houses, gardens back and front. **

There were two half brothers, Tony and Willy. I don't remember them arriving. They just appeared, or was it me? Was I fostered out, or just traumatised beyond memory? I must have been five years old because I started going to school, a big bright new red brick place where we had big assemblies and I had a green Plasticene penguin displayed on open day on the edge of the blackboard. My only other memories of school were of going in too early one morning because of some sadness at home. It was not quite light and empty schools are eerie places. The school caretaker took me down to his coke-fired boiler-room and gave me tea and a sandwich. I've always liked school caretakers. I suppose they are the only face of the "real world" in schools; door-fixing, fire-stoking, bin-emptying, problem-solving cheerful chappies. Thinking about it, I've taught in dozens of schools in England and Denmark and always got on with the caretakers. Maybe I'm just a pleb, or is it that somehow they carry the key to knowledge with their ancient bunches of door-locking devices and custodianship of the labs, libraries, workshops, echoing halls and classrooms of a thousand passing souls.

Council estate life in the '50s was a mix of tadpole fishing, field trudging to the summer-sticky, distant, disappointing, flinty mountain tops of the North Downs, discovering carpets of bluebells, gathered by the armful, dead on arrival, disappearing as quick as they came. Making unsuccessful perfume from rose petals, collecting useless clusters of acorns, capturing a pigeon in a box-and-string trap. The people – the Jones brothers lived five doors away with their docker Dad who had a telly where we would watch this funny guy called Liberace playing the piano in black and white on wet Sunday afternoons. Sometimes there would be the Lone Ranger and Tonto (with me trying to figure out how all those horses could get through the thin electric cable.)

Over the road I would play with Colin Richards who lived with his single Mum and elderly aunt and where the Bakelite radio was always on and *The Archers* coming on meant it was time to go home. We always had trays of cake for tea. They were foreign, Jewish, I would think nowadays, courteous and cultured. I enjoyed their kindness. One of our games was to go down to old slow line Merstraham station and stand on the bridge over the fast line from London to Brighton watching city gents flash by in bowler hats with briefcases and their furled umbrellas swinging on the corridor rail in the packed rush hour train.

There was a sister, Jaqueline. My older sister, Dorrie, appeared sometimes but I couldn't fit her in. In fact she had already left home aged 16. Jackie was the boss who told tales to my Stepdad to get me in trouble. He always seemed to be working away. He was into catering, working the country hotels and restaurants. Later he would commute back and forth to London, working The Savoy, Claridge's, The Dorchester, flunky floor-waiter and wine butler to the rich and nouveau-riche.

My mother did a great job on the garden and used to make cheese from sour milk hung from the kitchen windows in muslin. Colds would be cured by eucalyptus inhalations from a boiling bowl and a towel draped over the head.

I got my first car, a red pedal convertible with big wings. It must have been one of the few cars in the street because the only other vehicle I remember was the sweet bus, which must have actually been the mobile shop.

I remember my first real dealings with currency, four-a-penny Black Jacks, and my first mathematical tangle. The sweet bus sold my Hollywood hero cowboy "Roy Rogers" chewing gum.

"How much, mister?"

"Three farthings." I thought it was three halfpence so I couldn't have one with my one penny. There's four farthings to the penny, two halfpennies to the penny. The man laughed and gave me the gum and a farthing change. Twelve pence to the shilling, twenty shillings to the pound, that's 960 farthings. Wow! What a lot of Black Jacks for a pound. The big treat was Mackintosh's Rolos, thruppence, but they melted in the mouth and disappeared really quick into a creamy caramel heaven. So we used to buy Toffos; not chocolate, hard, chewy, but long lasting.

Years later as a post-university hippy, my mate Tim Cutting married Lizzie Mackintosh of the toffee family. I was best man at the wedding. I told her the Toffo/Rolo story. She gave me a box of 144 giant Rolos one year. I went round the streets of Islington over the Christmas/New Year cusp giving them away to surprised kids.

My first five-pound note was a short-lived experience. I had a small bedroom where I remember trying to say the prayers I had learnt at the new Sunday school, with good intent, but not much conviction. One night I was in my bed when this cheery, beery character turned up, gave me a bristly kiss and stuffed this huge piece of parchment under my pillow. It was an old, white five pound note, about four times the size of a modern fiver, probably the equivalent in value of fifty today. My Mum came later and relieved me of the burden of enough cash to buy 4,800 Black Jacks.

The man was Bertie Dowling, an Irish sweet millionaire who popped up in person or in conversation every now and then. I remember my first view of him was being taken to a roomful of scantily clad women in black negligée, overlooking Eros in Piccadilly. I recognised it, I was a central Londoner, born a mile away. Funnily enough I just heard on this morning's news about a flat for sale in that location for £1.5 million, maybe it was Dowling's old place.

My Mum's only 'holiday' was when she went to Ireland with Dowling and Co before my birth. I guess they must have been lovers. She was a Jean Harlow lookalike with a broken nose and a fiercely independent soul despite her three marriages and five children. She told me that Dowling said she was the only woman he could trust with his wallet.

Another poignant wallet anecdote was her talking about her time working as cashier at the Red Cross American Officers' Club in London during the War.

The aircrew would leave their wallets, photos and valuables with her when they went on missions over Germany. Some of them didn't come back.

"I never took a penny off those boys," she said, years later.

Bertie "fiver-under-the-pillow" Dowling's other claim to fame was as a gun-runner – probably for the IRA. My mother's basement flat in Victoria was used as a drop-off for crates of weapons, organised by her Scotland Yard "tec" chums as she always called them. Imagine, this was a blonde bombshell in her early twenties working the watering holes of the West End through most of the six years of the War, husbandless.

My Dad returned in 1947. He was a good-looking lad-about-town. Him and brother Paul had been twin page-boys at The Dorchester and professional darts "hustlers", playing the pubs for double or quits. I once saw Uncle Paul do a Shanghai, sticking all his three darts into his opponent's treble 18 as they were going for a double 18 finish.

Out driving late for Godfrey Davis he must have seen some post-war action too. In early 1947 they created me, making me a November 25th Sagittarian with Sagittarius rising, a post-war love-baby who grew up to be a life-long hippy and chocolate-munching womaniser!

By 1951 it was all over. My sister Dorrie, the love-child created in 1936 in Shropshire on a weekend visit to my Gran's hotel, was a teenage beauty. Continuing the tradition of child abuse he had been introduced to at his convent school and my mother's loss-of-father disaster at 16, my sister was sexually abused, seduced / introduced to sex by her father. My Mum found out – I can vaguely remember Victoria basement hair-tearing sessions with my mother screaming and assaulting my sister. It so happened that my godfather was Police Inspector Charlie Vanston, head of the "Sweeney Todd" (The Flying Squad at Scotland Yard). My Dad got given a divorce and four years in Wormwood Scrubs to boot. He always maintained he had been stitched up. He probably did get his sentence pumped up with a bit of help from my Mum's bent Police pals. Dorrie was incarcerated in a convent school.

This is where the stepfather came in. Denny, the Irish apprentice priest runaway from the seminary at Monooth, was the lodger. He swept my grieving mother off her feet and gave her two children in two years. Unknown to me I had got a new parent and lost a sister.

My mother wore the wound of the loss of her first love

throughout her life and never forgave her daughter. One of the last things she said to me, referring to the twelve grand she had stashed in coat pockets, bags, under the carpet etc. was "Don't give that woman a penny." She as a woman was still insanely jealous that her daughter had had sex with her man.

Three years on and re-settled on the brand new council estate in Merstraham, Surrey money was tight so Denny and Lottie/Mum took a job down on the coast at a hotel in Worthing. It was great for the kids because Granny Barratt was looking after us and she could cook fantastic food and cakes and bought me Roy Rogers's chewing gum.

My sister Jackie had developed a stammer. She always wore this green school uniform and she must have been about 14-15 at the time. She went to stay in Runcorn, Cheshire with my Aunt Lil, my Mum's half-sister and where they had all lived before the War. I'd been up for a holiday in their two-up, two-down terraced house, watching steam trains over the back garden wall. Uncle George, timekeeper at I.C.I., was always at work, but a kindly soul.

My mother told me not long before she died that my grand-mother had rung her at the hotel in Worthing and said she was going to leave us kids and go back to London unless my Mum agreed to Jackie being adopted by childless Aunt Lil in Runcorn. The reason? My sister Jackie was being sexually abused by my stepfather, Denny. What were those guys on in those days?!

I found the root of my father's problem years later; more on that anon, but the Irish seminarian?? Is there some innate male vengeance factor against his own progeny/stepchild when he arrives at the state of emotional and sexual redundancy? Children have been created, a nest established, the humdrum monotony of bread-winning existence has set in, the wife's love is transferred to the children, the exigencies of child and home care leave little time or energy for sexual love/pleasure and anyway procreation has long ago occurred. Why is this phenomenon of adults abusing their own children such an ongoing saga of revelation and accusation? Did Hollywood morality unleash sexual immorality /indulgence as a norm whereby the poor would indulge themselves within their own doors? Or has it always been there, one of mankind's most primitive rites, initiating their own children into sex, disguised under the moral stringency of Catholicism and its cousins?

The most telling recent comment I have heard is that it is the duty of he who calls himself a man not to pass the demons he inherited on to his children. That has a been the sum total of my fifty years + experience and residence on planet Earth. The social/economic pressures were obviously there in rural Surrey New Town. One time my mother disappeared for a week and turned up in a taxi with our first washing machine, a very early twin-tub model. Where had she been? Doing the scanty negligée scene with Bertie Dowling?

Another time my stepfather kicked the electric fire in a fury. It hit me in the face, chipping my front tooth permanently. He was apologetic, but what a shocker!

Soon we were on the move again, back to London in a dingy end-of-terrace with no back garden except for a World War II bomb shelter. We were in Battersea 1955. There was a single Ford Consul in the street and everyone was trying to master the Hula Hoop.

** *Years later, having written this book, I was returning from my step-mother Elsie's burial in nearby Redhill when I stopped at a village on the A23 London to Brighton road looking for a cashpoint. I realised I was in old Merstraham (on "the other side of the tracks" from the New Town. Some ancient instinct directed me to the wooden clapboard station still standing after all these years. I parked and looked up at a tree where I had seen my first nesting crows, walked into the station and over the bridge to the "other side". The old fast line bridge was gone, replaced by a tunnel. I emerged into a greenscape, backed by the rosy red-bricked council estate of quality 1950s British building. I walked up a grassy knoll and caught sight of the roof of our old house on Malmstone Avenue, the crest of the hill. To my left, where I remembered playing in squashy marshes and sampling my first watercress, the six lanes of the M25 motorway passed straight through our childhood playgrounds, and almost through our back gardens, where I had first seen Denny digging those red clods of earth. Here encapsulated was fifty years of the progress of the nation on the day the last senior member of my immediate family had passed on. As I stood contemplating this scen,e in the distance a man was walking his dog along the embankment that separated this past and present, a spindly planted tree was in the foreground and in a moment a brace of doves flew over either shoulder and settled on its branches.*

1955: Battersea

Black Boys and Savoy Style

Why did we move back to London? It turned out that my father Peter Goodchild, with new wife and child Noella and step-daughter Stella had moved to Merstraham, the old village on the other side of the railway tracks from the new estate. He had written two plays and was busy working with the Merstraham Players. One day he met Denny, me and the two brothers and Mum on East Croydon station. Denny wouldn't let him see me so he chinned him there and then – he was still chinning people at 74. I've got a vague memory of big green train doors slamming, shouting going on and often arriving home on the milk train out of Victoria.

My Mum was happy in the country, that's where she came from. Maybe it was the work (Denny, was yo-yoing to and from London), or the emotional pressure of having my Dad round the corner, but we packed up and moved back to sooty old London Town.

Back in Battersea we lived on a kink in the Evensleigh Road at No 174. It ran more or less parallel to the Lavender Hill. It was 1955ish and London was a black and white place after colourful Surrey. Germaine Greer once said the 60s were great because all the blokes started wearing colour. Before that everyone was in black and white. The back garden was all concrete but had a genuine World War 2 air raid shelter in it. Over the wall was an allotment. Being a post-war baby brought up on a diet of cowboy movies and war comic heroes I spent my time sawing out elaborate rifles and machine gun shapes from planks of wood by the old air raid shelter trying to imagine raining bombs, only to have the guns stolen from me by a near neighbour, a tomboy called Carol. Alternative activity was making bamboo bows and arrows with Kellogg's Corn Flake packet flights and firing them off at makeshift targets in the allotments, our city-boy countryside. One time my Mum bought us a 'wigwam' but it turned out to be an early frame tent that just didn't feel right stuck in a concrete backyard in Battersea.

My first Geography lessons came via mouth-watering moments in Mr French's corner shop. He always wore a white coat and a green Homburg hat. Eye to eye with tins of Jamaican treacle and Australian pineapple chunks I would ask what they were and imagined far-off exotic places. There was talk about Australia. British workers could still go there on the £10 Assisted Passage. I had a Jamaican mate up the road who I used to play cowboys and (West) Indians with. He always wore this hat with turned-down earflaps; poor sod was freezing.

I remember his house, stairs up to the front door which was always open, usually with some smiling woman sat on the wall, this and fantastic mouth watering spicy smells issuing forth. There was this silly saying about "niggers cooking curry in dustbins". One day I found my way to the back yard. It was small and bare of plants with a single, smoking dustbin.

"Yum yum," thinks I, "Time to sample some lovely food." I crept over and lifted the lid. It was scattered with the remains of burnt rubbish.

I reckon this cooking in bins thing is a throwback from National Service and the Empire. I was once in a mosque outside of Delhi at Eid, smoking dope with a bunch of Sufis. Outside the window was a cooking pot the size of a small swimming pool, big enough to feed thousands of pilgrims. These days I work the summer music festivals and when the punters have gone home I go to Mama Lynn's Caribbean Kitchen and sample some of her lovely goat curry cooked in a big stainless steel 'bin' – lucky me.

A big black bakelite phone arrived and Denny would be summoned to work the banquets at The Savoy, The Dorchester, Claridge's as an 'extra' waiter, wine butler etc. I came downstairs one night after being disturbed by adults. A grinning, sozzled Denny held up a full-sized lobster – never been big on shellfish ever since. Often we would get carted up to wait outside The Savoy Gardens by the river Thames for him to finish work. The excuse was that it was to stop him going into the pub. What happened instead was that we got left in the Savoy Gardens while they both went off to the pub.

The dreaded drink had always been a problem and we would have to listen to shouting and smashing matches whilst quaking in our beds. One night it was particularly bad with my Mum screaming. I crept onto the half landing and peeped round. A policeman was framed in the front doorway. Mum flew out of the back room and slung a cup at him, shouting "Fuck off, you bastard," as it shattered the skylight above his head.

23

Sometimes my Uncle Peter or Mum's cousin Cliff would stay. They were big red-haired, blue-eyed blokes with funny Northern accents who drove cranes and digging machines all over Britain and a place called Arabia. They would press half crown pieces into my hand whispering, "Don't tell your Mum." Years later Peter's son became a Premiership referee and reffed the game between Arsenal and Sheffield Wednesday, in which they had two draws.

Granny Barratt stayed for a while too and I'd help her bandage the big hole in her leg that would never heal, or help with the football pools. Later she moved out and went to work for Lord and Lady Cathcart of Cadogan Square, Chelsea. It was an upstairs/downstairs situation with her running the basement kitchen.

When times were really poor, that is when Denny had drunk all the money, I would be taken out of school dressed up in my blue mac, given a shilling and a small suitcase and sent on the 19 bus to Chelsea. Granny Barratt would sit me down to this long scrubbed wood table smelling of 100 years of baking and feed me some of her wonder grub. She once made dinner for a group of ex-Indian Army officers who congratulated her on her curry and asked her if she had ever been there! To India, Wales was the only frontier she ever crossed. She'd moan about Denny and Mum, stuff the suitcase full of food, give me an envelope with money and pack me off back to Battersea.

Another hungry excursion would be to the rag-and-bone man with papers or rags then I'd go and buy one shilling and sixpence worth (7.5p) worth of neck end of lamb from the butcher's on Lavender Hill, which would be turned into a pearl barley stew.

"We don't like this food, Mum," Tony and Willy would shout.

"Eat it up! It's Chinese food," she'd say.

Shaftesbury Avenue School was mostly fun. We did woodwork and I had this great teacher, Mr Matthews who was firm but friendly and came to school in an open-topped old banger of a sports car. He taught us about Phœnicians and Greeks and exciting far-off places as well as the usual stuff. Sometimes I would bunk off and play on the railway lines by Clapham Junction or buy a half-pound bag of chocolate drops.

I'd walk through 'posh' Battersea, through the park and up to the river Thames, that big muddy frontier, to where the really posh people lived in lower Chelsea. I was intimidated by the grand, six-storey private flats across the expanse of water and turned back with

24

my sticky bag of sweets to two-storey terrace land.

Football at Chelsea was a sometimes luxury but a long way off. Usually we would watch the reserves or the youth team with Peter Bonnetti in goal and Bobby Tambling and Terry Venables, later to become England manager. Many moons later, living in Brighton, my Uncle Fred's window-cleaning partner, Clive was doing night shift portering at the Brunswick hotel. The entire Chelsea team were staying there while training for the cup final. I was re-doing 'A' levels and hanging out with some girls from the University of Sussex. Clive asked me to get some girls for the party – not quite the right formula, Hampstead girl students of Art History and Russian and First Division footballers. (Funny how times change, now that Chelsea is owned by a Russian tycoon!) Tommy Doherty, the manager, was a memorable pig and Peter Osgood, England centre forward, still to be seen at the barely affordable Chelsea 'Shed' a real gentleman.

Even more years later I woke up in the arms of a lover with the Chelsea pitch right outside the window and a classy antique shop below. Not only had I crossed the tracks, but I had swum the river!

Runaway!

Early one summer Mum and Denny disappeared off to work in a country hotel in Sussex in the village of Alfriston. We were looked after by my older sister for a few weeks and then packed off on the train from Victoria. What a great adventure. We arrived at this old hotel outside the village next to a river with a couple of fishermen catching eels. It was lunchtime so we were parked out on the terrace while Mum and Denny served the meal. Of course, we were happy as spring bunnies bouncing around the countryside intoxicated on sunshine and scent of the summer flowers. We mooched about greenhouses and lawns with unfriendly sentry-like Leylandii trees whooping and hollering our childful fantasies. Suddenly my Mum appeared looking very pretty in her black waitress's outfit and lace pinny. But she was not amused.

"You are disturbing the hotel guests. Denny's going to give you a thrashing when he's finished." What did they expect? We had just been transported to one of the loveliest spots in Southern England with the river Ouse gently oozing by and the spirits of Normans and Saxons battling up from the beaches. Of course we were going to start battling imaginary foes and monsters with stick and stones. We were so pleased to be free of grimy back-of-the-railway-tracks London town.

I really couldn't take it, the thought of a black-faced Denny giving me a whack was like turning out the lights. I just started running – past the dozy fishermen along the river and into the woods. "Paul, come back," my brothers were shouting, but I kept running until I was in the dark of the woods. A road followed the river valley so I walked along it, keeping my eyes to the ground as I passed a solitary cottage. The trees thinned into hard, stubbly fields with scattered white flints. It was dusty and I was thirsty. The tarmac ribbon dipped into a lightly wooded vale and out of the trees appeared a massive smooth green mountain with a huge white horse painted on its side.

I toiled up the hot hill and crept through bushes to the head of the horse, my heart in my mouth, daring the 45 slopes of shiny slippery grass. It wasn't painted at all but close up was a disappointing tumble of white lumpy rock. I took a piece. It was just like the stuff Mr Matthews used on the blackboard.

The sun was on the horizon so I followed it through more cropped wheat stubble until suddenly a line of blue met the sky and I could see the sea naked for the first time. No Brighton seafront, no nothing, just land and sea. I stumbled on, more tired, more thirsty, more hungry, but knowing I had a shilling in my pocket. The sense of running away had left me. I was just out there at one with the road. It's funny, I've spent most of my life travelling since then and really the only place I feel at one with myself is on the move. That Sagittarian impulse to take one more step over the last horizon. I arrived in sleepy Seaford town and found the chip shop as it was getting dark. I queued with the customers, my stomach gurgling with gastric juices. Barely able to speak, I ordered some chips and reached into my pocket for my shilling. It was gone. I ran out of the shop in embarrassment and down to the stony beach in tears. The hero had gone out of me and I headed back down the road to Alfriston.

Luckily I got a lift and pretended I'd been to town for the day. I didn't want to go 'home' and face the music so I strolled around town looking at antique guns and the like in shop windows. A friendly bobby approached me with this strange helmet with a silver band through it.

"Are you the lad that ran away?"

"Er, yes, but I've been home, now and my Mum knows I'm back."

"I don't think so, son. Better come with me."

Dear Mum was so pleased to see me that any threats were dissipated with relief. I got put in a hotel room with a hot and cold basin and given the best roast chicken dinner I've ever eaten. Denny and Mum were still working and the brothers were asleep. Guiltily I tried to wash up the dishes in the sink but broke the plate and cut my hand. No, I wasn't dreaming. I had just been on my first adventure. Mum came in, dressed the wound, introduced me to the hotel owner and tucked the tired traveller into his bed.

A boy brought fresh field mushrooms in the mornings and we stayed a while, going for snake-avoiding walks in the woods, watching the hunt go thundering by and going on official visits to the White Horse, trips to Brighton and just a few weeks of school. I don't know whether it was Denny and the Demon Drink or having three kids hanging around the hotel but we were soon back off to London, all packed in a car and I remember that sense of disappointment as we headed back towards London with Denny boisterously pissed and my Mum crying a quiet tear.

She'd be pleased to know that I'm sitting writing this on a rock with bluebells to my left with the sight of a red setting sun playing wild horses with the clouds over a Spanish mountainside in the distance on a spring-blossoming terrace that 'belongs to me', as much as any part of God's creation can belong to anyone in the Sierra Nevada south of Granada.

Thinking of her!

1957: BATTERSEA

CLINT, CLIFF, CHIPS AND TV DINNERS

Life in Battersea was not that much fun but change was in the air and we got to have a black and white television and TV dinners, eating fried egg sandwiches as we watched Cliff and the Shadows on Saturday Nights and staying up late to watch Cagney and Bogart gangster movies. My mate Chrissie Boxer's Dad got a new grey-green Ford Cortina, the first car in the street and the girls started doing the Hula Hoop while boys crumpled in the gutter on borrowed roller skates.

What with Kellogg's Corn Flakes, TV, Ford motorcars, Hula Hoops and roller skates we were being truly Americanised and we loved it. July 4th was American Independence Day and us Battersea street kids heard that there was free ice cream in Battersea Park so off we went. All the Americans in London were there with a massive fun fair. We trudged around hot, tired, thirsty, skint. No free ice cream but suddenly I found a half-melted tub – there's nothing quite so anticlimactic as a warm ice cream. Skulking through the woods we spied on an American couple sitting down to a picnic with a crate of Coca Cola. We were Tizer tykes, we'd never had the stuff. A scruffy urchin went by "Hey, kid, have a Coke." Suddenly a tribe of Oliver Twists emerged from the bushes and did the whole crate before I could move. We traipsed round in a few more circles, the smell of roasting meat in our nostrils. There was a new America sandwich called a Hamburger that everyone was eating but we didn't get any. Later in the dried-up paddling pools I found my brother Tony, aged 5 with a Lucky Strike cigarette. The poor little sod was blowing it – logical, really.

I wonder if these are the kind of cheap experiences that Iraqi kids are getting 50 years later after all the expensive bombs.

MacAmerica Rules and the drinks R cool!

Drowning in Latchmere Baths

On Wednesdays we would go swimming with Mr Matthews in Battersea baths. I used to stand shivering next to the steps in the shallow end. Everyone else seemed to be swimming like fish. Out of school I went swimming with my mate, Dan who could dive and swim like an Olympian. Two things happened that would give me a fear of water, exacerbated by later events that would mean it would be twenty years before I learnt to swim and give me a lifelong dread of water.

First I decided to walk down the steps into the pool. The refractive index of water means that where there are five steps it will appear as four. I missed the last step and crashed into the pool gulping down chlorinated mouthfuls as I panicked and thrashed about. However, I was still up for learning to swim and the next week I watched as Dan did perfect dives from the edge of the pool. "That's easy," thinks I and attempted to execute the same smooth move. Halfway through the manœuvre I realised it wasn't going to work so turned the dive into a semi-jump and inhaled more mouthfuls of chlorine as I hit the pool. Luckily Dan saved me from drowning by pulling me upright by my hair.

Despite being good and keen at school I failed my 11+ and remembered Mr Lofthouse, the headmaster apologising to my Mum in his brown rolltop desk study. Lofthouse, that's funny, because Shaftesbury Avenue School has been turned into exactly that, £1.5 million flats and lofts for the nouveau riche Labour Party oppo's or webmasters of the New Era. I never found out what school I was supposed to go to because it was the summer hotel season again and we suddenly left the little terraced house that my Mum had been offered for £300 and we moved to Stratford-on-Avon.

"I should have bought that house," she always said. Now no local working class couples can afford to buy the million pound pads of Battersea.

1960: STRATFORD TRAGEDY

HAUNTED HOTEL

Ettington Park Estate near Stratford-on-Avon, the home of Britain's Most Haunted Hotel, this is where we went to live only it wasn't haunted then, only after the survivors left. More green and pleasant land for us to play in, me, Willy and Tony – in fact a whole aristocratic park land. Denny was the restaurant manager and Mum his helper and relief on days off. The mansion house / hotel stood on a hill overlooking the winding river Stour and the village of Newbold in the distance. It looked more like a French chateau with generous yellow stone arches and tall pointed turrets. It was the 12th century seat of the Shirley family, resident in Ireland since the 1850s and rented to Major and Mrs Reynolds. A ruined church with family crypt lay in the grounds and out the back a two-storey stable block around a courtyard, where we lived along one side, our back door opening onto a huge garden adjoined by the broken remains of greenhouses and a walled garden.

We became explorers, trekking through the woods, scattering birds, squirrels and rabbits, making bows and arrows, hunting down the 'enemy'. One day we found a tunnel made of limestone boulders partly fallen in. We edged down its dark curve, a light showing round the bend. Tony and Willy egging me on. Sun-baked foliage appeared and the tunnel opened onto a cavern. Suddenly three or four heads appeared and we jumped out of our skins, but they were only made of stone. We had stumbled onto a grotto with the busts of Greek gods cut in soft Jurassic limestone.

Later we found another tunnel in the side of a mound of earth. It led to a big circular stone pit full of the rubbish of dead branches and weeds with a high domed ceiling still made of stone above. It was a mystery why it was there. Years later, reading some Russian novel about alienated toffs hanging out in a country mansion they mentioned the icehouse and it clicked; it was an underground ice storage pit. More years later, tripping on acid I would find another identical ice pit in the grounds of Wivenhoe House, home to Essex University. Despite the illusion of grandeur living on our private estate the parents had to work and we had to start school.

Tony and Willy went across the river and over the fields to Newbold Junior School, a twenty-minute walk, on their own. It was safe in those days. I had to walk up to Ettington camp, a series of old Nissen huts occupied by refugee/gypsy families. I soon made friends with a quiet lad called Mick Reherling. He looked Spanish gypsy but his family were Irish and mostly sisters. Mick and I would travel on the school bus together, 10-12 miles, detouring round the country villages, to get to Shipston-on-Stour School, a brand new comprehensive school. Can you imagine that? Today these schools look like post holocaust architectural failures with their flat, perpetually leaking roofs, filthy windows, chewing gum engrained carpets and their illogical layouts. Back then they had a taste of newness and novelty with fresh green playing fields, airy corridors and serious teachers who kept us busy.

Being semi-Northerners, they played this weird game called Rugby. It seemed to entail lots of scrapping in mobs, pushing and heaving, loads of mud in the face and a ball that bounced all over the place and somehow one team would win – it took me ages to get the hang of it and even longer to get in the lower school team despite being really tall for my age. Later I found out why, I didn't have the right boots, just a pair of studded plimsolls.

The country girls were great and I spent a lot of time teasing them and getting threatened with the cane by the Deputy Head. Girlfriends and snogging didn't exist, they were just different, but nice. One girl I liked with red hair we picked up every morning from a big private Cotswold stone house with high walls. She was quite snobby, maybe shy, but there were others who looked down on the rest of us. Once in an Art lesson we were given the task of painting the sea. One girl was really upset. I asked what the matter was.

"I've never seen the sea," she said.

The library was brand-new and the thirst for knowledge very much alive from Mr Matthews days and anyway, we didn't have a telly any more. I took so many books out of the library that the library teacher grilled me on their content when I took out three in three days. We had a very strict teacher and at the end of the term he read out the results of our tests and class work. To my amazement and embarrassment I came top of the form, ahead of the nice but snooty auburn-headed girl. From then on a kind of competition took place between me and her which I guess with time would have become a kissing thing.

The "Adventure Playground" of the Ettington Park Hotel and its grounds was a bit secluded. On days off we would go into Stratford which would invariably end up in some hotel/pub with us having a meal and Denny embarrassing us by being pissed. Other times we'd go out on the pleasure boat by the Stratford Memorial Theatre. We didn't really have an idea who Shakespeare was but he must have been important because lots of Americans came to see him.

There was a great lady in the bus station who could pour twenty cups of tea all at once out of a giant silver teapot. One day we got the long, hot double-decker bus to Oxford but as soon as we got there we had to turn around and come back again. I suppose it's the same these days after the great era of timetabled buses and trains to obscure destinations finished when Thatcher and her pals sold the family silver of public utilities owned by the people for the people. I once asked a manager in Bristol bus company how anyone would get to Stroud after privatisation. "Stroud? Stroud will cease to exist. You're nobody if you ain't got a car."

One result of this Shakespeare thing was that an actor called Patrick Allen lived in the lodge house at the bottom of the drive, a big booming geezer with a square jaw like Desperate Dan and cheeky blue eyes. He was always flying by in his Aston Martin open top sports car. My Mum used to clean up and cook a little for him and I would help out with carpentry jobs. She told me that once she went down there to find the remains of a very drunken party, bottles and glasses everywhere. Jack McGowan was gone to the world in a four-poster bed. She went to wake Patrick. There was a lump in the bed with him. He took it by the hair and yanked it awake.

"This is my friend Peter." A handsome blonde-haired thespian opened twinkling blue eyes and declaimed, "Lottie, oh Lottie, I need a woman like you. Please, please come and be my housekeeper." It was a young Peter O'Toole.

Being explorers we kept agitating to be taken out in the hotel boat which lived in the stables below in the back of an old Land Rover. It was made of aluminium with twin floats and unsinkable. Denny kept putting us off and anyway he normally only had Mondays off and that was reserved for getting pissed. The periodic battles between the parents were getting worse, often at night, but also during the day

33

and evening. In the middle of the flare-ups he would often shout "Goodchild, come here!" and my Mum, with a fearful look would say, "Go to him." I'd usually get some demeaning task to do, a clip round the ear or be called greedy for eating too much. I didn't know what he was going on about.

My name was Denny, who was this Goodchild? The only memory I had of a Goodchild was when my Gran used to point to an old man sitting on a balcony in London and say, "That's Godfrey, Goodchild's father."

After one particularly bad night of fighting and yelling when it seemed the oak beams in the bedroom were part of a pitching ship my Mum came to my bed and whispered, "Paul, I've got something to tell you. Denny isn't your real father. Your real father's name was Goodchild."

I've had plenty of time to think about this in my aimless wanderings about the planet. Lottie Barratt ran away to London aged 17, pregnant, to join Peter Goodchild, the man with the come-to-bed eyes as she called him. He was a sexual loose cannon. Him and his twin brother Paul had been twin bum boys to High Court judges (my Mum once went for one with a Gurkha kukri when he came round to their flat mistaking Peter for Paul), chauffeurs to twin gay stock-brokers as well as Hollywood style dandy/charmers around the London scene of the 1930s. Still, she loved him inside out and had three children, Dorrie, Jackie and myself. Even after getting him the four years in Wormwood Scrubs and sending Dorrie off to a convent school, she still loved him, taking me on unremembered prison visits while married to Denny. I was the sole survivor of this love, a perfect blend of the two characters in physiognomy and temperament, a post-war love child nurtured on National Health nutrients as I grew too big for my boots, literally. I was getting to 6 foot aged twelve and the first boy in junior school with long trousers. I became an object of hate and jealousy for Denny.

Every Monday that springtime of 1961 he would have a day off while my Mum worked at the hotel. I would arrive home last on the school bus. He would be sat in his armchair near the back door in a black post-lunchtime drinking session mood. I would have to make my brothers' tea. Whenever I tried to be creative he would say, "Stop that, give them bread and butter." So we would sit down to this measly meal in a gloomy silence with him glowering from his armchair.

One afternoon my mother came back and said, "What have you had to eat?"

"We only had bread and butter," I said.

"What d'you mean 'only'?" shouted Denny as he launched himself across the room at me, his right hand smacking me across the ear in a thunderclap of pain. This treatment was repeated every Monday and became an inquisition. He would get me to stand by his chair and answer a series of questions until I got the wrong answer and then whack me with a backhander across the face without moving from his chair. Then I'd have to stand there again for a repeat performance.

I'd had enough of this treatment and decided to strike back. There was a big cut glass decanter in the hallway and I moved it to the window ledge right behind his bald head ready to whack him with all my might in one knockout blow. They did it all the time in the movies. I can't remember any fear, only an overwhelming feeling of necessity, like having to mix cement, to make mortar, or carry water from a well, climb a hill to reach the top, a matter-of-fact example of pure survival.

That Monday April 12th 1961, I got home mentally prepared to do battle. I came through the back door from the garden. A ghostly silence fell like a spell across an empty room. Sun slanting through the courtyard window onto a perfectly set tea. Glass bowls of mandarins, neat triangles of sandwiches, and a Battenberg cake. I went to the door and looked out into the empty courtyard.

The boat with its unsinkable floats was missing. Maybe Willy, Tony and Denny had gone out in it. I decided to go round the back of the hotel and down the drive to Patrick Allen's to see if he needed a hand, that way I could see down to the water as well. As I came level with the front of the hotel my mother ran out of the front door screaming. I ran over. She was on her knees.

"Quick, quick, the boat has turned over." I ran down the drive towards an old iron bridge and looked down the river. I could see something floating fifty yards away. I hacked my way through bracken and tried to climb a spindly sapling. It was no good. I ran back to the bridge and along the grassy meadow bank by the water.

Denny was dead, floating upright in a sitting position, his bald head touching the surface, thin hair floating in a halo, exactly the target I had been measuring for my lethal attack.

A hotel worker came. My mother was hysterical and taken away. The Police came and frogmen. It took two days to find my brothers in the tangled weeds of the deep mature twists of the river Stour, while we held out hope that they might emerge somehow alive. Denny had died of shock when he hit the water. The two brothers drowned. How did it happen? Why did it happen? They say that nesting swans were with their young and could have attacked the boat. It was unsinkable with its two floats either side, so it's the most logical explanation. Denny with his usual disregard for his inherited stepson had taken his two sons on the river before I got home from school, leaving no friendly message. Thus I was saved. Why? That's anyone's guess. I haven't moved the earth or any mountains apart from rebuilding a rustic ruin in the Spanish Sierra Nevada. The only thing I have really achieved is to share in the rearing of two children without passing on the bad karma that was handed down to me by the spirits.

Thirty years later I returned to the spot with my good friend Leslie Turner to place my mother's ashes in the same river where her sons died. The mature river had become a muddy ditch floating with agricultural effluent too shallow to drown a cat.

We went to Alderminster church and placed the box in a shallow trough, secretly and silently in the spot where I reckoned my brothers were buried and marked it with a solitary goose-feathered arrow.

And the Haunted Hotel? We went for tea at the Ettington Park and picked up the brochure – "Britain's Most Haunted Hotel" – haunted by the ghosts of two children of the Shirley family drowned in the river in the middle ages. Funny how myths are born.

A strange epitaph occurred on my 48th birthday. I came downstairs to breakfast to find a card from my elder sister Dorrie. Inside there was a photo of me aged 12 kneeling next to my brothers' grave with a huge white lily in my hand.

Later that day I went to an exhibition of paintings by my friend Luke Piper in London. I didn't know at the time that he was grandson to John Piper, impressionist painter specialising in churches and 'Ghastly Grange' historic homes as well as being a famous stained glass man who had done the windows in Coventry Cathedral. I picked up a brochure of his prints and turned it over. On the back cover there was a painting of the Ettington Park Hotel done from across the fields near Newbold. The foreground was the exact spot where my brothers had died. When I came to publish my first book

"The Blue Angel Quest" (dedicated to my dead Mum who made it possible with the £12,000 she had left stashed under carpets and in old coats) Luke kindly let me use a blue and gold iridescent painting of the church window of Stansfield by his grandfather taken from the front of the same brochure.

1962: LONDON

SINGLE PARENT CHILD

We buried my two half brothers, Willy and Tony and their Dad 'Denny' in Alderminster graveyard on the road to Stratford-on-Avon. Mr and Mrs Reynolds the Ettington Park Hotel owners invited Mum to stay on. As a servant, she had nowhere else to go. They had given up the council house, forfeited their chance to buy the house in Battersea for £300 and now she was homeless. There was no way she could stay on in the idyllic setting of Ettington Park with the ghosts of her dead sons ringing in her ears. Being a single parent in the 1960s was not the relatively cushy number it is today with full benefit and the £130 a week rent paid. Nor was there a cultural "fashion" of single parenthood to provide solidarity. The expression 'Single Parent' had not entered the dictionary. That was the work of my university contemporaries in the 1960s – middle-class feminists who could afford to live without men and knew about birth control. My Mum was a homeless widow with an 11 year-old child. She got a pension of £1-25p per week and no rent paid.

We headed south to the cities again, stayed first with Mum's red-haired brother, Uncle Peter in Coventry, where the new cathedral was just being completed.

I remember my mum buying my first charcoal-grey suit in a cheap clothes shop in a smoke-stained back street.

He loved her but she was devastated, working in some crap hotel and hitting the bottle. Auntie Brenda and her had never got on and older cousin Kieron loved bullying me. I went to one of the 13 schools I would notch up and got punched in the face straight away by the biggest kid in the year group. I couldn't understand it and I was rightly scared. After a week or so I had had enough so I belted him so hard with my one good punch that I still remember the look of surprise on his face. Coventry fell apart and we ended up in London sleeping on my Gran's bedsit floor in Victoria. The geezer upstairs took a fancy to me, showing me photos of being a ball boy at Wimbledon while putting his hand down my trousers, luckily, just as my Gran walked in.

A 'Pad' in Victoria

I remember during this itinerant time being in London with my Mum around Victoria with nowhere to stay for the night. It must have been gone 12 o'clock and Mum stopped to buy me some milk from a milk machine. There was a feeling of desolation, emptiness, apprehension and ... that eternal thread of hope. A man younger than my Mum, maybe in his twenties came to get some milk and started chatting.

Ten minutes later we were in his tiny basement flat, crowded with bunk beds in the corridor, low lighting and a small messy table. It was an early bohemian/beatnik pad that I would find easy to recognise today. I lay in the grubby bunk bed reading some naval yarn he gave me while Mum sat up and chatted through the night. The next morning, back on the road with our bags. Mum went to get her widow's pension and by some miracle they paid her twice. She took me straight down the market and bought me a new pair of shoes and a slap-up breakfast. Homeless and penniless, save the widow's pension, Mum got a barmaid's job in a pub where she could live.

She would never find it difficult to get work. She had Hollywood good looks, charisma and peroxide blonde hair as well as being born into the catering business. She could do it all, cook, clean, cocktails, chambermaid, receptionist, cashier. When she was about thirteen my Gran left her in charge of the Red Lion while she went to market.

A man turned up in a touring car and asked for the landlord. Mum explained they were at market and offered him lunch. He accepted and sat writing notes in a small book. After his food he asked for his bill and made to leave. Mum said, "Don't you want to wait for my mother and father, they will be back soon."

"That's not necessary," he replied. "I am from the Automobile Association assessing your hotel for inclusion in our guide. I am so happy with the service here I'm going to give the hotel a three-star rating.

So when she got the job in the Greyhound pub in West Croydon High Street, they were the lucky ones.

WORLD WAR 3

I moved in with an old school friend, Johnny Grenfell and his family and for a while enjoyed a normal life and went to school. William Blake, it was called, near Battersea Bridge Road. It was a secondary modern with an over-the-top uniform in maroon with blue piping and a cap quartered in blue piping.

We had a headmaster Dr Rudd who taught us Latin and who would fly about in his gown threatening us with the stick but it was still quite a wild place. I remember having to biff some more bullies there who tried to beat me up.

One day Johnny told me the world was going to end. There was going to be a nuclear war and we would have to stick brown paper bags on the school windows to save ourselves from nuclear radiation. It was the time of the Cuban Missile Crisis. Kruschev wanted to place missiles in Cuba and President Kennedy wouldn't have it and threatened to send naval vessels to attack and escort Russian missile ships. It was a tense standoff with hands on the pistol butts of nuclear Armageddon. Kruschev, who had been in charge of the siege of Stalingrad, knew the costs of war and backed down. We were saved.

The climate of fear as it is so strangely called is a purely man made phenomena and it is suddenly as strong now as it was then. There was this constant prickly dark sensation of the end of the world in our young minds a bit like the fear of all the collected unknowns that a young mind dwells on. The propaganda about the Russian threat and the Cold War was a constant theme in the media of the day. Was the average Moscow school kid really plotting the overthrow of the West and sharpening his penknife ready?

The root sensation of this notion of a threat to our post Kellogg's cornflake civilisation is actually the same as that gigantic existential question mark that we all eventually ask, *"Who am I? Why am I here?"* or *"What is your purpose?"* as the Indian roadside enquirer so neatly puts it.

These essentially spiritual questions are subverted by our material masters to sustain their position as the lords of an industrial machine the engine of which is driven by the technological advances in the highly profitable production of weapons of mass destruction. A neat linguistic switch that swaps prophet for profit. It is more like the politics of mass distraction.

I once studied with a real gentleman of a Scot called Jock English. He was an ex Royal Navy helicopter navigator. He had toured the Pacific been on manoevres in Norway, flown over Iceland in the Cod Wars and retired to a guaranteed retraining place and a cottage in Dorset. Jock was not the kind of guy who gave off even a hint of aggression or intimidation. However he and millions of others on both sides of the Cold War divide had spent 30 + years getting paid for playing with some of the most advanced technology known to man maintaining the climate of fear. A recent MOD announcement tells us of joint NATO manoevres with the Russian Navy and my old football club Chelsea is owned by a Russian!

Johnny and I got on with life kicking balls around Clapham Common drinking bottles of flat Tizer and playing car recognition with the dozen or so makes of English motor car; Sunbeam Talbot, Rileys, Hillman Hunters, Singer Gazelles, Ford Consuls, Vauxhall Wyverns, Jaguars and the occasional Rolls Royce. I would go up to the Red phone box on the Common and make my first phone calls ringing my Mum at the hotel pushing 30 mm discs of old Imperial copper pennies into a big black box with buttons A and B and holding the heavy black bakelite phone in two hands.

I hadn't really cried over my dead brothers but one morning I went into the Bathroom and Johnny was submerged under the soapy, milky water his hair floating just like my dead stepfathers.

'Johnnnny!!!' I screamed.

'What'? he said rising surprised from the deep. A couple of days later I burst into tears and sobbed over Willy and Tony but not Denny.

It was time for me to move again and I went to stay with the Jones's, our old neighbours in Merstraham, Surrey.

Old man Jones was a hard but jovial bastard. He worked the docks in London and always came home with something different and drunk boiled stinging nettles for his arthritis. There was a dart-board in the back alley where I remember getting hit by darts thrown by the sadistic younger brother Davey.

Saturday afternoons we would get the disgusting job of worming tin baths full of whelks. Imagine a snail in its shell that lives under water and is really slimy. You pull out the body with a pin, squeeze it and dig out the 'worm' (its intestines). Urggh – it's the worst experience I can remember, hours of it, hand covered with this dry slime cum shellfish diarrhœa. Old man Jones would do a great trade down at the council estate pub on Saturday night. Sundays we would get taken to the seaside in his Bedford van with sliding doors open, always to this grey shingly beach at Dymchurch where the sun rarely shone. How aptly named.

GOODCHILDS AND BADDADS

Soon I was on the move again. My Mum picked me up in a taxi one night and took me to a bar/social club up at Heinemann's Press on a large country estate in Surrey. We were going to meet my Dad for the first time. Of course she got a bit pissed, as usual. He was manager of the social club with old-style threepenny-bit fruit machines, massive billiard tables and a cosy bar. I remember sitting in the taxi outside crying my eyes out with pure emotion ...

How do you say to a 12 –year-old, "Oh, by the way this is to your Dad?" In the here and nowness of time there was no thought, just feeling.

He was blonde-haired, blue eyed, like me, with a Bohemian pointed beard. He had read about the tragedy in the paper and had written to my Mum. He lived in nearby Woodhatch, next to Reigate in a small cul-de-sac council estate with a giant lime tree that left the pavement sticky. He had a wife, Holly and a stepdaughter, Stella, a bit older than me and a 3-year-old angel called Noella, my half sister. He was mad keen on growing runner beans and we had them with every meal. Mum was still working in the hotel near Croydon and had a boyfriend, Tony Jackson, who was a nice guy and a bit of a wide boy. So I stayed with my Dad and his new family and for the first time had my own bedroom and started school at Reigate Priory. My Dad took me along for the interview and introduced me as Paul Goodchild without telling me! Suddenly I had a new name and didn't like it. Not least because all the kids started calling me Badchild, BadWoman etc., which was hard to take for a 12-year-old who didn't quite know who he was or where he was. School was cool and I enjoyed it, but the boat of cosy domesticity and family life was about to capsize again.

What happened was that Holly went to see Mum because she felt threatened by her. The story goes that Jackson, the new boyfriend, and Mum got her pissed and tried to rape her. Next thing Jackson and Mum turn up in Woodhatch and there was a massive punch-up with Dad banging Jackson's head on the concrete steps by the front lawn. It was back to battling and screaming time. Holly left and went to live in Liverpool with her kids.

My Dad once described my Mum as half devil, half angel, and it's true she could get her hooks into someone and not let go. There was a very intuitive and possessive streak in her that would not back off, particularly when pissed up on gin. (I've even had my hands round her neck on one occasion.)

Around this time when it was all going wrong I awoke one night to this booming voice shouting, "For God's sake, Lottie!" as the house shook. It was my Uncle Fred punching the wall. He was a lovely burly, bearded Burl Ives lookalike, ex-actor, ex-stage manager, retired with heart trouble, window cleaner in Brighton. I went downstairs and met him for the first time. He had come to adjudicate and try and sort out the mess. I never regretted one instant of knowing that man and had the privilege of kissing his head as he lay in his bed dying of a brain tumour years later.

"Wotcha, cock," he would say whenever I walked through his door as he reached for the frying pan to cook me some grub.

Life settled down a bit and I met my father's twin brother Paul for the first time and his eight kids. I'm a fairly full-on character myself these days, but eight Goodchilds living in a council flat in Paddington was so intimidating. Pauline, Pete and Pat were at work. Slinky Cynthia was full of love and teased her frigid cousin. Howard was my age and good at school, Roger and Vicki, the twins, slightly younger and dear Penny, bless her departed soul, had a hole in her heart and Down's syndrome.

Auntie Bess was another of those faultless people, always at her kitchen sink. Half the mums in the tower block would call by as she was on the ground floor next to the lift and, like Uncle Fred, would always get the frying pan out when she saw me walk through the door. I would sit amongst my boisterous larking, micky taking cousins tongue tied and be so intimidated and embarrassed that it would take me hours to pluck up the courage to say "Ah – hmmm, er, I'm going now!" Mostly I stayed with my Dad and visited my Mum at the hotel in Croydon via long bus rides. He started having these weird guys round. Soon he got me to sleep in his bed and started to introduce me to sex. Of course, at first it was pleasure and I liked it but it soon started to feel all wrong.

I went to stay with the London Goodchilds for a bit but then he turned up and took me back again. This time there was a sense of dread. My life was a mess. My Mum was just about keeping her life together in between getting pissed to drown her sorrows and my father was seducing me.

1962: ROYAL INFANT ORPHANAGE ASYLUM

I used to read comics and in particular followed a strip called *Sandy Dean's Schooldays* all about the jolly pranks the boys at boarding school got up to.

It seemed such great fun. Next time I saw my Mum I said "I want to go to boarding school." Somehow, it happened. We went to County Hall in Croydon and they found me a place in the Royal Wanstead School, London E11.

The Royal Wanstead School was still called the Royal Infant Orphanage Asylum on the London A-Z maps when I went there in 1962. Today it is the London Law Courts, and during the Second World War, an Italian prisoner of war camp. It housed about 250 senior boys and 120 mixed juniors. Someone described it as a secondary modern boarding school run on public school lines – all of the disadvantages of both!

Purpose built under the patronage of Queen Victoria, it looked the Imperial part, designed by the same architect as St Pancras station. Dormitory and teaching wings flanked four grand grey stone towers with castle-like crenellated walls fronted by a huge playing field and an ornamental lake. On the very edge of east London, surrounded by Wanstead Flats and touching Epping Forest, it was as green as you could get and still have a London address.

I arrived walking with my suitcase, accompanied by my Mum. A long drive of overgrown rhododendron curled up to the visitors' entrance and a set of wide steps.

The aura of Victoriana was everywhere, long cloistered corridors, polished floors, a grand marble staircase leading to the Governors' Rooms, flanked by oil paintings of past luminaries, dormitories with cast iron beds and green blankets, a dining room with ranks of 12-seater tables and a raised dais for the headmaster and prefects. A giant chapel with spectacular stained glass windows and a colossal new organ.

I was soon stripped of my identity and issued with my day, Sunday and very best school uniforms, which meant third-hand, second-hand and new plus two grey shirts and two pairs of shoes. I got given a buddy, Peter Spreadbury, because he came from Surrey, and was stuck in form 2b as I had missed so much school and was deemed a bit thick. I soon came top of the class by about 200 marks and went up to the 'A' stream.

There were four houses, Churchill, Babylon, Nineveh and Athens. There was that Winston Churchill again. He was the local M.P. When he died a couple of years later we joined the thousands passing by his coffin in the Houses of Parliament. I was stuck in Churchill house with the demon house master John Davies who loved whopping our butts with the cane, alternated by giving us his psycho "how-dare-you-exist" stare.

My two best mates were Mike Hammond (bless his soul) who would stay a lifelong chum and gentle Mick Sly. Two ancient nurses looked after our laundry, toiletries and issued black blocks of Derbac anti-nit soap. Situated over the kitchens, we would get awoken at 7.30 by the smell of fried bread wafting through the windows. After breakfast we would sweep the dormitories under the supervision of monitors and dorm seniors and our house prefects who got to wear very best uniforms all the time and were demigods who were either very brainy or captains of various school teams.

The curriculum covered the usual academic spectrum plus Woodwork, Metalwork, and Sports, including sailing on the lake, which I would have loved to do but no way, due to the fear of water and the dead brothers. Some of the teachers were good, others, like John Davies, bullies and some just unsuited to the profession. Mr O'Gorman was obviously a clever boffin but bored us to tears with Physics. Mr Williamson, our Biology teacher, a wide boy northerner, spent most of our Biology lessons telling us in great detail about the books he was reading; Ian Fleming's early Bond adventures!! He was also a piss artist and a sadist who once whacked me across the knuckles with a brass-edged rule. Bert Knight, the completely useless Woodwork teacher who ran the Cadet Force had us making one teapot stand in four years (while waffling on to his Cadet Force keenies instead of teaching us)!! Funny how, twenty years later, I became a woodworker and Technology teacher despite Mr Knight.

They say that in school you will have two teachers who you really like and communicate their subject to you. M.P. Davis was one, John Butlin the other, both very different characters. Mike Davis was an ex-paratrooper and cross-country running champion with friendly blue eyes despite his hard, wiry exterior. He was so tough that not only was he the Three Peaks champion but he had beaten two Ghurkas from Nepal on the Ben Nevis race with a broken ankle. He was ruthless in his determination to shove geographical information into our dozy adolescent brains. After a lifetime of cerebral abuse I can still walk into a rowdy classroom of kids I've never met and mesmerise them with my map drawing skills while entertaining them with tales of my travels inspired by M.P. Davis's introduction to World Geography. I have actually hitchhiked to Yemen via Italy, Libya, Egypt, and Sudan and into Ethiopia and Kenya and driven overland to Sri Lanka! (and am writing this halfway up Spain's highest mountain).

John Butlin, our English teacher, by contrast, was a Wildean dandy who dressed in hacking jackets, drainpipe cavalry twill trousers, check shirts and cravats if he could get away with it. He was ex-Cambridge with a haughty public school accent and wicked wit. He lived in a plush flat nearby with his equally dandyish toff chum, Richard Williams. I would later become their cleaner/manservant during 'A' levels, earning pocket money and snaffling water biscuits with strange cheeses, Gentleman's Relish or strong marmalade snacks. Richard once pronounced that the worst thing he had ever done in his life was to save David Frost from drowning while at University

I loved English but hated grammar and clause fucking analysis. John Butlin was always castigating me for writing war stories, but I would end up getting the top English grade in the school in my fourth year with a tale of a bicycle courier in the Second World War! Since then I have self-published a book of poetry and two novels and entered into correspondence with MPs, government ministers and various luminaries in my quest to start alternative boarding Life Skills Colleges, not to much avail, apart from disseminating ideas on the virgin but barren ground of political and educational change in the UK.

My love of words and travel have always helped me unravel the curious kinks in the unstraight street of life. My thanks to those two teachers and their teachers!

The intake of Royal Wanstead School consisted of kids in care for one reason or another plus the sons of minor missionaries or NCOs in the forces. There seemed to be a plethora of single parent kids. Winner of the smallest muscle measuring competition, my mate Leo "Stringbean" Turner's Dad was killed in a Lancaster bomber in

France just after the war. Mick Hammond's Dad had died young and there were many other examples. We were all wards of the state, our fees paid by the local authorities and topped up by our working mums. Years later I would find a tear-jerking letter from Surrey County Council thanking my mother for her £3-a week contribution to my fees. Imagine the loneliness of that poor woman, mother of five, one flown, one adopted, two dead and the last in boarding school. No wonder her constant friend was a bottle of Gordon's gin.

She would come to visit on Sundays with her new boyfriend, a Geordie truck driver for Pickford's, who was a steady, zero-imagination, linguistically incomprehensible guy outside of everyday conversation. At the time they were living together in a room off the ugly Holloway Road, two souls in trouble making it a double. He had bought her a bottle of gin one night when she was drowning her sorrows in a local boozer. They stayed together for the next 35 years. He had been fatherless too. Down the mines at 14, joined the army at 16, fought the Japanese in Burma, been a military policeman in Calcutta, fiddling punters and prostitutes alike and sending a small fortune home. Sergeant Miller arrived home in Chester-le-Street, County Durham and found his kids shoeless at home and their Mum down the working man's club with her lover. He found them and beat them both senseless, leaving them both for dead. He went and reported himself to the local Police station. The Police sergeant said, "You'd better go home, Billy, man. The blankets in the cells are wet. We'll come for you in the morning."

He got four years in Durham nick, headed south afterwards and became a loner lorry driver for Pickford's doing 18 day stints away from home until he met my Mum.

Strange that many moons later I should run an "alternative" removals business "Goodmoves", running furniture for socio-economic refugees to "drop out" destinations all over the U.K. and Europe. Billy only taught me one thing in his Geordie English, but it was a life-saver: "If you're driving long distance at night, man and you're tired, get your head down for five minutes and start again." These words have echoed back to me many a time halfway through a 26-hour non-stop drive to Spain, or back and saved my cross-eyed neck

Eventually Mum and Billy got a "flat". Two rooms with cold water on the landing over a junk shop in Highbury's Blackstock Road, a few doors from the Arsenal Tavern, where Billy would prop up the bar doing his regulation six pints of Guinness a night after a hard day's drive. Mum was working a city snack bar, the Bodega Tavern and I would sometimes work there in holidays or visit, going on interminable walks around the city, pretending I was some young businessman on a mission.

The underlying sadness of her situation was always there despite her fundamental optimism – she was a long way from the countryside now but decorated the flat in green floral wallpaper, made a bedroom for me in the back, a bed sitting room for her and Billy and a kitchen on the landing. He was still going away on long distance missions so she would get left on her own and hit the bottle on the way home from work. Often on school holidays I would sit between the two of them like a referee. Her back early pissed-up on gin, him back late pissed up on Guinness, plates of dinner flying across the room hitting the new wallpaper, gravy running down the wall. I would be so pleased to get back to the dark Victorian corridors of the Royal Wanstead and the camaraderie of my mates. My Mum's visits became less frequent as I became more interested in my burgeoning friendships and started treating her as a sweet-and-goodies provider for me and my chums.

The bullying was a big part of life at school and as usual big boy Goodchild was a natural target.

On my first night during prep – compulsory homework sessions – I was putting my books in my fold top orphanage desk when this guy Tim Watson gave me an almighty thump behind the ear. I'm quite a placid guy until I get upset and then a black destructive rage takes over. I slammed shut the desk and smacked Tim Watson in the face. Luckily a mess of chairs got in our way and the fight was broken up.

"Right, I'll see you later."

"When?" says I and I arranged to do battle before breakfast the next morning down by the lake. I got up early full of butterflies but determined. Matey boy chickened out and didn't turn up. We spent the next two years ignoring each other except that he never bothered any of my puny mates again. There is always a pecking order in schools with the older boys pushing the younger boys about. I was a natural target because of my size, but one day I'd had enough when a senior boy started pushing me about. We started the chest-shoving scene. He wasn't one of the worst bullies and I quite liked him but soon we had a crowd egging us on and it turned into a full-scale fight.

I was being backed up against the wall when I gave him a back-handed punch across the face. There was an awful cracking noise and his broken nose spurted blood all over the corridor. I had to see the Headmaster that time round and I got four light lashes of the cane. Later the fifth form gave me a form 'session' beating which was more terrifying than painful.

He was a lovely bloke John Lavender, our head, an old-school Oxford man flying about in his gown with a big booming voice. He loved driving around in his Singer Gazelle car and he had this Princess Margaret lookalike slightly wasted-looking chain-smoking wife and I detected a certain sense of emotional sadness in the man. Later, when we were seniors he would take us for current affairs and tell us stories of his own pranks as a boarding-school boy. The Royal Wanstead was a successful institution in that it gave stability to 250 young souls away from their dysfunctional childhoods. On the other hand it robbed us of a "normal adolescence". There was no street life or community outside of school that would sustain our progression to adulthood. Once school was over there was no sense of "home" outside of the total institution, nor any girls to play with!

SEX AND THE BEATLES

The only females were the kindly matron with a face like Mother Christmas, some ancient nurses and the nice Welsh Miss Owen who guarded the food supplies and her friend Linda who looked after our clothing needs. Latterly German girls came to work as au pairs and were present at serving and clearing up after meals as a nice distraction from the bland grub. They all lived in attic corridors above the boys' dormitories.

My first experience of sex was with a local girl. By some miracle the public came to a bonfire night celebration and I met this girl from nearby Woodford. She invited me to visit her. She was a foster child and her parents were out. We ended up in the bedroom where she immediately exposed her fulsome breasts! – I can't say I really knew what I was doing, but I liked it. It was innocent enough and exciting. School holidays, the exigencies of boarding school life plus her undoubted appetite for the opposite sex ended our relationship. It would be another couple of years before I lost my virginity, got into the 6th form and started to find my way around the school after dark.

Being the early 60s social life was dominated by the telly and the transistor radio. The Beatles and Gerry and the Pacemakers were on the grainy black-and-white communal TV. Top of the Pops listened to on hot Sunday afternoons down by the lake on the school playing fields or stuffed under our pillows after lights-out. Of course we all bought guitars and tried to emulate Cliff Richard and the Shadows. I saved up and got a bass which I used to amplify by pulling the head off the school record player and stuffing the wires in. I'm not a natural musician and am much to short on patience to learn something that isn't obvious, like music or languages.

By the third form I was starting to spend my holidays in different places: on Cadet camp trudging through the ferns of Sussex with hot blanket-wool uniform and a .303 rifle with blank cartridges, trying to chat up girls in the local choir: the Isle of Wight on Scout camp, building a tent of twigs and rushes, lying awake all night waiting to batter invading snakes, the Scout master in his tent marking 'O' level English papers! Staying with my sister Dorrie and her first husband Ben in Reigate and doing a milk round. Sometimes, but less and less, with Mum, riding across London on my second-hand bike, following lorries through the Blackwall Tunnel to visit schoolmate Mick in Croydon. Hiking across London to visit the Goodchild tribe.

51

1964: Goodbye Gran

The truth was I didn't have any friends or social life outside of school at all. The jewel in my life during school years was Granny Barrat. She'd settled in some sheltered housing off Tooting Bec Common – a converted mansion with large airy rooms overlooking a garden with a fruit-bearing mulberry tree. I would go by tube or ride my bike from far East London to far South West on my thrice a term Sunday leave-outs, or during holidays. I would often tell her when I was coming but even when I turned up unannounced she would have my favourite lemon meringue pie and triangles of cucumber sandwiches set out in a perfect display of culinary art.

I would often sleep on the floor in front of her fire and she'd tell me stories of the old days. She still had this huge cancerous hole in her leg that had to be washed and bandaged everyday. One night she started crying and said she wished she was dead and how no one would remember her after she was dead. I comforted her and told her I would never forget her and I never have, nor have I laid flowers for any of my dead relatives, my life's been far too itinerant but I've carried them all in my heart and my actions and had two kids of my own.

One day in the 6th form John Lavender, the head called me to his special office up the marble stairs to tell me in his gruff, apologetic voice that my dear Gran was dead. I burst into tears right there and walked down the stairs past the painted ancestors of the Royal Wanstead School in a state of desolate shock. My consolation was that I had seen her in hospital the previous week and told her that I had finally passed my resit Physics and got a grade 1 in a self-taught Divinity 'O' level, which pleased her no end.

CHORISTERS, CADETS AND CRIMINAL CAPERS

Boarding school was a bit of a prison, really and now it really is a prison as the East London Law Courts. We had Saturday and Wednesday afternoons 'leave-out' for one hour, two hours on a Sunday. We had this super-creepy discipline-master called Bill Star who hated my guts, probably 'cos I wouldn't shag him like some of the other under-age boys in his supposed care. He used to cruise the high street on his bike making sure we were wearing our caps and school uniforms with a clipboard on his handlebars. It makes me laugh at the reversal of attitudes later. I'm in school these days and have to ask kids to take their rude boy caps off!

There were several ways of getting out of school. One was to join the choir and go to concerts, another to join a school team. I ended up as captain of cross-country running as I was so useless at the skill sports – that was hard work!

Cadet courses was another.

I can actually remember sitting on a 19 bus in army cadet uniform with a live .303 rifle between my knees feeling a bit awkward en route to a drill course at Chelsea Barracks ... what chance that these days?

In the 6th form all my mates joined the choir, not because they were Christians but because they liked a good singsong and going on the annual bun fight to Brighton. In fact good old Leo Turner was such a committed atheist him and Mick Hammond used to have cross-burning sessions on the rifle range. Once we went to a huge choir convention in Chelmsford Cathedral which was a nightmare because most of the other choristers were natural songsters, unlike me. As a Royal School we wore red cassocks like King's College Cambridge, for example. There was a golden moment as we stood in our tight red full length outfits leaning nonchalantly on the cathedral columns as hundreds of girl choristers trooped by looking at us as if we were some sort of demigods of song – good job their sweet voices drowned out our grumbling quasi-bass-baritones.

Cadet force was a drag. We had to endure it twice a week in our blanket-wool uniforms marching up and down with our Nazi schoolboy C.S.M. John Enright. I was so pleased when he screamed at me one time to put my knees together. I couldn't because I'm bandy-legged and he crouched down furiously trying to push them together.

I ended up teaching map reading, which was tolerable, but repetitive. It was 20 years since the war and we were still practising trench warfare and flanking the enemy with infantry manoevres. Ha Ha Ha. It was at the height of the Cold War and we should have been burrowing towards Australia collecting brown paper bags to absorb the radiation flash and learning the basics of cannibalism for when the food ran out!

One minor claim to fame and the beginning of my career as a faceless extra in forgotten televisual events was when Field Marshall Lord Montgomery, the hero of Alamein came to see us. I expect he was licking his lips at the chance of sending us off on a massed attack of the Russkies when they came over the Channel. The event was filmed for BBC news and we crowded round the TV for our split second of glory.

I managed to scrape eight 'O' levels, much to my amazement and together with a half-dozen pals decided to stay on at school mostly because there was nowhere else to go and we knew nothing about the outside world at all. It was the Royal Wanstead's first proper 6th form. The trouble was that they only offered Geography with M.P. Davis, which we all loved, and music and art. We had to go to the local High School to top up the rest. I ended up back with John Butlin who had moved on but I could never get my head around the joy of endlessly studying the meaning of Milton, Shakespeare or Chaucer and anyway there were girls in the class who I was always trying and failing to impress, needless to say. I failed 'A' level English miserably and it was such a misery to study. Times were getting modern. We were half way through the 'sixties. I found out that they had all these interesting courses at the local Technical College in Walthamstow and I persuaded the head to let us go there.

I managed to do two one-year courses in Geology and Economics and get a largely self-taught B and C grade. With six periods of Geography with MP Davis. for two years and the related subjects I should have gone into orbit but I knew so much I could never finish an exam and ended up failing it at the first attempt and with it the opportunity to go to King's College, London.

Anyway, as 6th formers we were starting to have some of that *Sandy Dean's Schooldays* fun I had been seduced by years before but hadn't yet experienced. We were given a 6th form room in a small building stuck on the end of the gym way out across the parade ground and backed by the corrugated fence of Epping Forest. It was an ideal opportunity for me to practise my hobby of chasing girls. Me and Fudger Wilson, who used to win so many events on sports day they had to limit him to two, decided to build a hidden den-cum bedroom in the lost triangle between the 6th form room, the gym and the forest. Mick and Stringbean joined in because they had got a motorbike they wanted to hide there. We needed bricks and mortar so we used to bunk out of school with rucksacks and nick them from building sites. Fudger got himself an illegal scooter and took me on a full-scale raid to get a decent amount of materials. We broke down the fence to a building site and loaded the back pannier with a box of bricks, filled up my rucksack and then he wanted to get a bag of cement. There was the two of us arguing about this bag of cement, him pulling one way, me the other until it broke all over my groovy Black Magic Man velvet trousers. Panicking with guilt I made him start the scooter up, jumped on the back with my rucksack full of bricks. The front wheel lifted right off the ground heading for the moon. I walked back to school hiding in doorways.

Another time we decided to nick an old school blackboard from the boiler rooms under the school to make a roof. Imagine some kid looking out of the window at 6 o'clock on a summer's morning and seeing an eight-legged blackboard walking across the playground.

Eventually we were found out and good-natured John Lavender let us off, but made us knock down our knocking shed/motorbike workshop.

I had lost my virginity in the back of a ladies' hairdressing salon the previous summer, so I was now a fully qualified crumpet-hunter. I started to go on excursions to Epping Forest pubs with nice Miss Owen, her Thames bargee boy friend and Linda who ran the sewing room. She was a pretty lass from Rochdale, Lancashire and I was soon invited for brief, fearful skirmishes in her tiny room in the garret of the school. She left later that year and I tried my tricks on the German au pair girls. I went out with one of them for a while but she was a good girl and always wore very tight white jeans and didn't want to make a mess of them. Big-eyed, blonde, buxom Lee Jordan worked with the infants and she was an enthusiastic snogger and grinder who used to drive me mad with frustration, but I was keen enough to go and visit her parents in Deal, near Dover, one holidays.

Halfway through our relationship she decided to take up with my old black running mate Percevon Boyer, a proper Jamaican kid who was a great runner and very easy going. I would be team captain. He would always win. I'd be second except for when I secretly trained and plotted to beat him in the school mile. He was furious and wouldn't shake my hand afterwards. He'd actually left the school and when Lee started going out with him. I was insane with jealousy and racist tinted rage.

She came back eventually and we settled down to our elongated snogging sessions until the Head caught us in the 6th form room at the beginning of one holiday. She kept her job but we had to stop seeing each other.

My true love was a girl called Valerie Shaw who I saw very little of as she lived in distant Lancashire. I met her when we went on a field study trip around the Yorkshire Dales with MP Davis – us trudging over endless tussocks of swampy grass, lunching on Kendal Mint Cake in the mist and being amazed by the 2,000-foot mountains that he kept running up and down in training for the Three Peaks Race. I had never seen a mountain before, only the rolling bosom country of the South Sussex Downs. We stopped at different youth hostels every night and they were hale and hearty places crammed with keen girls from northern grammar schools on Geography field trips. We set up a competition to see who could get off with the most lasses. I managed to win, being the most rehearsed of our group and I set up a pen friendship with Valerie.

She was a great big-eyed lass who wouldn't let me get away with any bullshit. Every holidays I'd hitch up to see her in Accrington, travelling all night up the new M1 and M6, stopping off at old style transport cafes for pints of tea and bacon sandwiches. We really loved each other. She sent me wonderful pink letters, heart-shaped homemade shortbread biscuits. Once, and this was actually before the one-night-stand virginity losing session, we were snogging down by the river and we were both so hot and moist that I said to her in this stammering voice, "Val, do you believe in sex before marriage?"

"No," she said, shoving me away. I saw that girl for two more years, hitch-hiking up to see her and she even got herself a university place in London to be near me. Our relationship degenerated from that ecstatic moment onwards and I was cast off in the role of "only wanting her for sex", despite hitchhiking from London for two years and not doing it! Eventually she wrote to me about this guy Ross who she was seeing who was much older and more mature. It was obvious that she was having sex with him. Luckily for my ego, I was having sex too.

I'd left school and joined some evening classes where I met a deliciously beautiful, slightly Asiatic-looking German girl who taught me all there was to know about sex. She was actually the daughter of an army general from Munich but reckoned her father was probably the milkman! I wonder what Monty would have thought about that!

Finishing with Val was the end of first love for me and I've never found it ever again in my entire life despite several illusory episodes and embarrassing infatuations. It was the kind of psycho-trauma that my lack of family life and boys' boarding school existence left me singularly unable to deal with. I expect it's true to say that I've treated women with a fundamental emotional icy-hearted disrespect ever since.

Meanwhile my sensible chums in the 6th form were aiming at much more achievable targets. Apart from their cross-burning escapades on the school rifle range they set about rifling the school pantry and organising mammoth eating competitions. There was Fudger Wilson and Mick Hammond shovelling wedges of ham, sponge cake, baked beans, and then forcing pineapple rings out of seven pound tins into their swollen cheeks. Mick won, out of sheer bloody-mindedness rather than physical ability.

The school belatedly opened a tuck shop. Fudger Wilson, the athlete found a way in by standing on a radiator, cocking his leg over his head through a tiny skylight window and somehow sliding in his shot-putter's shoulders through the gap. I was spending more time swotting in the library and the prefects' room than in the 6th form room with its Who and Rolling Stones music belting out.

I foolishly handed over my locker keys. When I turned up on one of my rare visits a month or so later the lads went all mysterious on me when I asked for the keys back. I later found out it was stuffed with stolen food and tuck.

One night a pale-faced Fudger woke me up – I was the acknowledged expert at nocturnal excursions, leaving my bed stuffed with pillows, dressing gowns and a football to make it look, to a slightly pissed house-master on his way home from the pub, as if I was dreaming away.

"We've been caught on the roof of the school by the headmaster."

"What were you doing?"

"We were trying to find another way into the tuck shop." I was appalled. I didn't even know they were burgling the tuck shop – or that they were hiding the swag in my locker. I was also really knackered from a prolonged snogging session in the woods. "Oh, just tell him you were looking for lost tennis balls. You're keen on sport," and went back to sleep.

Years before we used to have this game of bouncing balls off the ornamental turrets of the school until we lost most of them. Good old John Lavender believed them but they were really stretching their luck and there was no stopping them. By this time Fudger Wilson had bought himself a 3-wheeler Messerschmidt car and motorbike. Mick Hammond was his accomplice. Another protagonist was Geoffrey Knebel, a red-haired, cravat-wearing con man with an affected public-school accent and mannerisms. For weeks the rest of the 6th-formers had been bursting into song when they saw me, a version of Elvis Presley's "I'm Crying in the Chapel" changed to "It's raining in the chapel". I knew they were up to something but couldn't work it out and they were in stitches. I tried to find out. Unfortunately for them the school staff found out first. They had nicked the lead off the chapel roof, lowered it by rope, put it into Fudger's 3-wheel motor and flogged it down the scrap yard. Mick, Geoffrey Knebel and Fudger all got expelled by a now furious John Lavender.

Being goody Goodchild I came back for the second year 6th fully expecting to be Head-boy. I had some great ideas about changing all the unnecessary line-ups we had, relaxing the rules on school uniform and making the place less Victorian, more relaxed. To my disgust John Harrison, best pals with nasty Bill Star, and still struggling after two years to pass his 'O' levels, got the job. The Head apologised, saying that Mr Star had refused my appointment. Six months later, Star and Harrison were both caught at it and were sent away immediately.

It was too late for me. I was past caring. I had already lost my house captaincy by taking my entire football team off the field when the referee, Mr Dimsdale, whose house we were playing, tried to send off our best player. "Bailey off," says he. "Churchill off," says I and off we all went. Mr Dimsdale! How aptly named. What with the politics of hot bollocks and the love rejection I was ripe for revolution. I just didn't believe in the old school ethic anymore. It was the beginning of the end for the decent John Lavender era. The new school staff were low quality piss artists and the 60's were upon us.

Dave Godfrey, the lad whose nose I had broken earlier turned up one day to visit his brother, looking really cool in faded jeans and told us about his travels round Europe working in vineyards, busking, playing music. This sounded exotic and perfect.

I had tried really hard to make the grade. In the 4th year I wanted to be a boy entrant in the R.A.F. By the 5th year I upped my sights to becoming a pilot. That way I could travel and support my Mum. I went for Officer Aircrew selection at Biggin Hill with boyish dreams of dogfights with the Hun in the Battle of Britain in my mind. First I failed aircraft recognition/co-ordination tests, then this eighty-year-old doctor with what looked like a miner's lamp on his head looked in my ears and said, "I don't know why you bothered coming here." The final humiliation was being sent into a completely black room.

"Right, what colour's that light?"

"What light?" A tiny pinprick of light appeared in some remote distance of darkness.

"Erh, white..."

"Ok, what colour's this?" The same pinprick of light.

"Red," says I, thinking they must have changed it.

"This one?"

"Green." I kept guessing. Luckily for me. I was totally unsuited for supersonic flight and, as a pacifist, ended up in pole position carrying the Essex University banner outside the American embassy, protesting the Vietnam war in 1968 and supplying food and drink to the key speakers and stewards at the anti Iraq war rally in London's Hyde Park in February 2003!

I finally set my sights on being a development economist and applied to do Geography at King's College London. My first 'A' level Geography failure was followed by post-school resits, first obtaining an 'O' grade and then finally a 'C' grade and I ended up doing Sociology and chips at brand new concrete ivory tower Essex University in 1967 ripe and ready for the sex, drugs and rock and roll revolution that was about to happen to me and hundreds of thousands of other teenagers across the world.

CRAP YEAR – GAP YEAR

The end of 'A' levels and academic failure co-incided with the end of life in a total institution. Mum was still living with Billy Miller in the two-room flat in Blackstock Road. I moved to Station Parade Romford with my mate "Stringbean" Turner and his brother who he didn't get on with and called Ogre Boga! Also resident was Alan Trinder, our old house captain, studying architecture and living with his girl friend, a strait-laced Teutonic lass from boarding school au pair days. String and I used to cook feasts and adopt Italian accents while cooking pasta etc. Once we had a tinned roast chicken! It was set over a parade of shops. The rooms were tiny and as we were big we slept in a row of single beds all crammed together.

Our mate Bobby Smith, whose Dad was American, moved in and the Beach Boys became the dominant music. Pete and Dud and *That Was The Week That Was* were our favourite viewing on TV. Nights were long and mornings were short. We were free of boarding school régimes. String invented new times of day: the Swaghtling was from about 11am to 7 at night, the Nachtling 7pm to 12 in the morning. Little did he know that the future would spread the urban population away from the eight-hour day towards the 24-hour day. Who would have thought then that supermarkets would destroy corner shop culture and stay open all night to accommodate an expanding population an increasing number of whom would have to live a semi-nocturnal existence so there would be enough room for everyone to fit in!

September came and I enrolled at the hardly-ever-heard-of East London College of Commerce in Aldgate to do some more 'A' levels after failing to get into the R.A.F. and King's College. I had to try again. I started out with Geography and British Constitution – a new, bigger, non-subject than Sociology. I was elected social secretary but there wasn't any social life in Commercial Road, East London in those days.

My Mum had moved over the road from 141 Blackstock Road, so I moved into my own flat with Bobby Smith. That didn't last long before we started arguing about the cost of corn flakes. He was a super-meticulous guy and I'm a broad sweep bungler. The problem with the new pad was that my dear Mum was still trying to mother me, the surviving member of her family of five, in between still drowning her sorrows and doing on and off battle with Billy Miller. Apart from the sex education with the German lass it was hell. College was crap, Islington was a dirty hole that had yet to become trendy and I didn't know a soul apart from people I didn't want to know like the landlords of the local pubs.

The low spot, literally, was getting this giant carbuncle-like boil on my chin, which hurt and made me look like Quasimodo's younger cousin. On top of this I heard my long-lost sister Jackie had a baby in distant Runcorn, near Liverpool. I had a three-boiled-egg breakfast and hitched up there in the snow. Arriving at a forlorn, colourless council estate after an all-night journey, sister Jack looked at me and said "You can go right back where you came from!"

Years before my Mum and Bill had trained it up overnight to go to her wedding to Derek, an artificer at ICI., where Uncle George had worked all his life. He was her first sweetheart and she had lived with childless Aunt Lill since she was thirteen. Now in her early twenties they were mother and daughter to the locals. My Mum, turning up with Hollywood good looks, blonde peroxide hair and a fur coat slightly upset the proceedings and got tongues wagging. Jackie had written to her afterwards saying that Mum had ruined her wedding and she never wanted to speak to her again.

Considering what our mother had gone through with the loss of her husband and sons, that was small-minded and vicious. I could see where it came from, that small town jealousy of the charismatic and attractive. At thirteen years old I wrote back saying that Jack had been influenced by 'that evil woman' Auntie Lil. She hadn't forgiven her little brother and when I turned up on her doorstep three years later to see my namesake she shut it in my face.

My Dad had started writing to me while I was at school and I had gone and secretly stayed with him after my GCEs and told my Mum I was staying with a school friend so as not to upset her. He had settled into a new life with Elsie, a dressmaker, in Hove Sussex. I had ridden my knackered push bike with all my worldly possessions bulging in panniers nearly all the way to Brighton before he met me and picked me up. He was working doing a window-cleaning round with Uncle Fred and between them they knew a lot of people. Desperate to get out of the sad flat at Blackstock Road and away from bleaksville I asked if I could stay with him and Elsie. My dear Mum had tried in her way to provide a flat for me in London. In those days it was a £2-a-week Church of England property that was cheap, unmaintained and Dickensian. Now it's probably worth a million and a half.

I got all my mail redirected via my old school mate Mick Sly so as not to upset my Mum and moved into a cupboard at my Dad's place in Hove. Elsie, or Elise, as he liked to call her, ran a dressmaking business in one room. They had a bedroom and a massive front room, beautifully done out with my Dad's decorating skills. I used to sleep on the floor and disappear my existence into a cupboard every morning. Those Japanese with their foldaway Futon beds don't know how lucky they are.

I got a job working on a building site across the road, as a labourer. By now it was 1966 and both Engelbert Humperdinck and Jimi Hendrix were on Top of the Pops. Sussex University was the new hip place to be with the Jay twins, daughters of a Labour minister, personifying the supposedly new classless Britain. Brighton was also full of sexy foreign language students. Meanwhile I was still trying to get to university, sitting through long afternoons swotting and gawping out the window at the lovely Swedish au pair girl sunbathing next door. King's College had kept repeating their offer until the second time, when I only managed an 'O' level pass.

Damien Pugh, my mate on the building site smoked dope but I had never heard of it and it would be a good year and a half before I first tried it and another 25 years before I gave it up! Damian lived with some ex-art college mates in a Bohemian pad on the sea front, where they made painted dolls, or something. It all seemed very cool and confusing to the ex boarding school boy who had tried to join the Royal Air Force I started going to student clubs and gigs.

Once I ended up at a Chuck Berry gig at Sussex University. I was standing on my own trying to feel trendy, watching the warm-up band, the Graham Bond Organisation, Dick Heckstall-Smith on tenor sax, Jack Bruce on bass, Ginger Baker on drums (two of these guys would later become Cream, with Eric Clapton). I turned round and this seven-foot-tall black guy with twinkling eyes was standing next to me.

"Hello, Mr Berry ..."

"Well, hello there, son," he said, sticking out a massive right hand for me to shake.

Later in the evening I ended up with a lardy da lass from Chelsea with horn-rimmed specs, nice body and super-short mini-skirt, being given a lift home in her Triumph sports car. I stroked her knee. My rough builder's hands caught in her stockings.

"Er, I'm sorry ..."

"It's rather nice, actually," she purred. – I didn't know what to do or who I was, stuck in this netherworld, six years in a boys' boarding school with the fire crackers of the 1960s exploding all around me.

My Dad worked as a porter at a posh hotel and despite being the author of two published plays sat and watched the telly most of the time. He thought with my quasi public school upbringing I should be a hotel manager – wrong plan. I had just bought myself an orange shirt, a pair of bell-bottoms and made myself a fur waistcoat out of an old coat and was about to meet Sandra Judson of South End Green, Hampstead, graduate of the Camden School for Girls, studying Russian at Sussex University and whose Dad was a liberal lawyer and friend of the murdered true leader of post-colonial Kenya, Tom Mboya, with a mother who worked at the Citizen's Advice Bureau. I was about to have my poor little brain twisted by the middle-class intelligentsia.

1967: Sussex University

I met Sandra over a kitchen sink at a party. She was looking for somewhere to wipe her hands. "... use my jeans ..." We went home together and soon started shagging. She lived in a shared house with her mate Sarah Gathouse who was doing Art History and whose Dad was a left-leaning ex-big shot in the National Coal Board. In fact there was a whole house full of Sussex University girls and it was a kind of liberal heaven after six years of Victorian-style boys' boarding school, the hell-hole of Highbury and sleeping on the old man's floor.

I soon got carted off to Hampstead where I became a bit of a working class hero with the Judson family and friends, what with my dysfunctional upbringing and building site occupation. The 1967 Arab-Israeli war was on and of course I supported the underdog and followed the pro Israeli propaganda in the newspapers. Sandra's Mum, home from the Citizens' Advice Bureau Office in Swiss Cottage and having her evening quadruple sherry, gave me a full-on lecture about the politics of the Middle East.

Sandra and I slept together in her bedroom at her parents' house, opening onto the garden and her parents didn't mind a bit. When I later tried the same manœuvre on my Dad's floor the mild-mannered Elsie hit the roof, with accusations of 'dirty sluttish behaviour ...' the lot. I got invited to the Gatehouse's country pad in Sussex. They were pals of Michael, later Lord Young of Dartington, one of the pioneers of post-war socialist engineering of which I was about to become a beneficiary. I got used to eating informally with a fork only and great French-style meals with tossed salad. I'd never eaten a salad before a meal or after and I had to adjust my boarding school table manners.

We were in the middle of the 1964 Labour Party's first term and the talk was all about social policy, the dead hand of Conservatism and a class-bound society was collapsing under its own weight and these people, the student generation of the 30s and 40s were now in power, helping it on its way. I was mesmerised and the combination of kindness, intellect, nice places to live in Hampstead and Hampshire and winsome daughters meant I was definitely not getting back on that 19 bus back to bleak Blackstock Road.

I was about to become a déclassé person stuck between the past and the future both free of social label and free of a sense of belonging. It was a liberating and lonely sense of non identity that would propel and compel me thru the rest of my life living on the margins.

With Sandra studying Russian and seeing herself as the political commissar of the New Left I was always getting it in the neck for my petty bourgeois reactionary attitudes. We had a blazing row down the pub when I sided with people who were getting shot for jumping the Berlin wall. Sandra tried to convince me that they were traitors to the communist state.

I enjoyed the debates and high-minded talk and it was time to start thinking about my own university place. I liked Sussex but I knew I could not get a place because I did not have a foreign language. Eighty per cent of good universities would not consider someone who did not have a language. Because I had missed a whole year of school and we had a very meek French teacher who later committed suicide I was sent to the library instead of doing French. It is the biggest regret of my education that I do not speak any foreign languages.

I have delivered furniture to rural locations all over France and lived there for short periods. Not speaking languages is the same as not being able to swim and being stuck on a beautiful beach. Luckily for me a ring of new concrete-and-glass, as distinct from redbrick, universities were opening around London; Kent, Essex, East Anglia etc. I applied to all of them and decided to drive around them in an old Ford van to explain my imperfect qualifications.

I had bought the van off my Dad's garage. Trouble is, I couldn't actually drive.

My relationship with Sandra had fizzled out as it was the summer holidays and she had gone to Russia or Poland or somewhere. I met a nice French girl called Mirielle Echeverria from a Spanish Basque family living in Paris who liked having sex with me and she could drive, so we went on a tour of all those universities near London. I had a confirmed place already secured at the Newcastle College of Commerce and thank God Essex University said OK, you can come and play here! Funny I should get a French girl to drive me around to explain my lack of French!

I spent my summer holiday in Paris visiting Mirielle and her family secretly sleeping in their garage, spending a night with an old madame and her young Algerian prostitute and visited a Brigitte

Bardot lookalike I had met in Brighton called Evelyn Meunier and ate classic French lunches in a musty old room over a courtyard with her grandparents. It was my first experience of a continental culture that I've never lost the taste for. Perhaps one reason for this British obsession for French and Spanish culture and cuisine is that it is more rooted in its traditions than us British with the amorphous influence of our empire and the headlong post-war Americanisation of our civilisation.

1967: Essex University

Wivenhoe Park, a stately home painted by Constable stood on a hill over a muddy river outside of the squaddie town of Colchester, famous for being burned down by Britain's first feminist, Boudicca. Its old school charm had been swamped in a sea of concrete and glass. Hundred-foot podia supported interlocking paved plazas, a giant four-storey library block with giant brain-frying windows, ugly serrated concrete finish wall and a constant action cyclical lift, loomed overhead as if it was going to batter us with knowledge. Fourteen storey tower blocks built in dark grey engineering bricks stood off on the once-green meadows. A lot of the staff had been head-hunted from the London School of Economics, 60s hotbed of radical intellectuals – Essex was sometimes called LSE. in the country.

Professor "Positive Economics" Lipsey, Peter "Chairman of the Fabian Society" Townshend, Alasdair "I think therefore I am" MacIntyre, Michael Meacher the drop-out minister from Tony Blair's government was a junior lecturer. Unlike Brighton it didn't have a Bohemian underground culture or a student tradition – we had to make our own. We were the third intake, little thinklings from the planet thought dropped on the Essex marshes next to a market town on the way to somewhere else, famous only for its squaddies and its military prison.

Initially I didn't have a grant and lived on a diet of chips, gravy and yoghurt bought in the weirdly shaped hexagon restaurant. I shared a study room with a working class girl from Kent. It was in one of the tower blocks and in a flat that contained study bedrooms as well. We used to sit in there with a dictionary trying to decipher all these weird sociological terms and getting behind with our work. Because I was doshless and there was a flat full of utilities, shower, kitchen etc I soon started dossing on the floor. The 14 storey tower blocks were gender sandwiches – boys/girls, boys/girls. Good old Professor MacIntyre the philosopher and Dean of Students decreed that we could not have overnight guests of the opposite sex in study bedrooms. However, you could have overnight guests of the same sex. I don't think he was gay but he was definitely discriminating against heterosexuals!

There was always a party going on and lots of coupling up and cross coupling. Hendrix was still knocking it out, Cream were riding high, Deep Purple, Led Zeppelin, Roy Wood's Wizard, the Who, the Stones and Oh yeah! Oh yeah! the ever-present Beatles. There was a small posse of long-haired purple-cloaked oddballs and their frilly girl friends who listened to some atonal outfit called the Incredible String Band and another musical mess called the Pink Floyd while floating a foot above the ground with knowing smiles on their faces. I was still padding around in blue jeans, white baseball shoes and American air force leather jacket looking like a south coast art college hipster. Another bunch of misfits went around in grubby raincoats or overcoats and steered well clear of me and my trendy cohort, levelling drunken insults whenever they had the chance.

One of these characters was another man/boy called Turner - Martin. Despite being very opposite characters we ended up becoming lifelong pals. Martin's speciality was surliness and destruction combined with too much drink. Him and his pals kicked in the milk and cigarette machines in the launderette so many times that they were taken away. These guys were mostly clever and a cross between Northern working class lads, like Howard Jackson and Hugh Someone-or-other, the filthiest of them all, whose Dad was a famous university professor and author. Their collective identity was anarchist delinquent. We were supposed to be studying, in my case first year Social Studies, Economics, Sociology, Philosophy, Computing, Spanish and Something Else.

I had taken up seeing Sandra again in Brighton and was commuting for long weekends in between sleeping on floors and living on the chip line, which meant missed lectures. I was already behind given that 95% of the students were a) bright b) had been to proper schools c) had normal parents and a home income they could fall back on. My Mum was still stuck in London settling into life as Billy Miller's faithful slave and always keeping a bed for me that I hardly used. They had moved to 114b Blackstock Road, a one and a half up and one and a half down 'cottage' at the end of a cobbled lane next to Pickford's warehouse where he worked. I always stayed in regular touch. My Dad wrote me a really encouraging letter after kindly putting me up on his floor for 6 months:

"You've become a bum, son. You're not welcome here any more. The welcome on the mat will be reversed when you grow up and become a man!" Nice one, Dad, you just pulled the mat out anyway.

Poor guy! He'd never seen any of his four kids grow up, had assaulted or sexually abused most of us and was so busy mimicking his conservative masters in the hotel trade that he had no idea how to cope with the avalanche of social change that was about to happen.

Not long after my Uncle Paul, my father's twin, gave me the elbow when I jokingly referred to getting a dose of VD. Getting the "clap" as we called it, was part of the rites of passage of coming of age in the permissive 60s. He banned me from contact with his family, all of whom, I would later learn, he had sexually abused. I was on my own on a frontier of personal, political and social change that would continue for myself and succeeding generations up until the present time.

'Normality' was gone. Change had become the norm.

I finally got my grant through at the end of the term. I moved into Wivenhoe village with a bunch of lads who I still know today. John Dunningham, Rob Wombwell and John Bradley. Dope smoking had just been invented and John used to go to Brixton to score. He also ran the blues club, Rob the folk club and I got left with the handful of people who were into jazz and a £50 budget for the whole year. There was lots of music about and even more chaos. I didn't even smoke dope or cigarettes and I thought they were all slightly demented, particularly when they started rolling about on the floor laughing their heads off. I seemed to be the only one that bothered with sweeping or washing up.

In the Christmas holidays, with nowhere to go, I took a job working at Butlins in Clacton making hamburgers and doughnuts. The mass entertainment scene was not my cup of tea. I distracted myself by getting off with a 'normal' girl, from Ilford. There was this life-changing moment as I was walking along Clacton sea front with her at 8 o'clock at night with this big neon Butlins' sign blazing across the horizon. I was trying to describe what smoking dope was all about and realised I didn't know because I hadn't tried it. Being a committed sociologist I decided to gather some empirical evidence and try it next term. It would be another 25 years before I gave it up.

Life got really confusing then, but it was fun. I could now make sense of the weird Pink Floyd music. Wivenhoe village was rocking with dope smoking, music playing students. Johnny Etheridge, later to play with Stefan Grapelli and end up with his own jazz trio had switched from guitar to alto sax and could be seen waving like a dervish in his bedroom window making a horrible squeaky noise.

A bunch of middle class graduate women slung out their husbands and started the first issue of a magazine called *Shrew*, (later *Red Rag* and finally *Spare Rib*) Britain's first lesbian, sorry, wimmin's magazine. The rock and roll revolutionists and the femino-libido liberators rubbed reluctant shoulders and went in the same political direction.

Two atypical students were Pete Jocelyn and AN Other, two Essex Constabulary Police inspectors who were both in my study groups and I got on with both of them. A few years later Pete went on to become chief superintendent of Colchester nick when I was still floating on the margins of what had become the English East Coast Scene. He was good enough to see me one day and warn me of my impending arrest for non-payment of a fine. He later became Chief Constable of Warwick. Fair play to him! I can remember him taking on a hall full of radical students with his common-sense arguments – unlucky him! Passion and reason are poor bedfellows, but essential companions.

His colleague gave me some cash jobs in my first term – being a traffic man he told me how the Police drivers used to train not using a clutch. It would be a life-saver nugget of info years later when I drove a second-hand post office van from Bombay to Goa through the night with no clutch.

With all this see-saw psychic yo-yoing going on the studies were getting lost and I had to settle down. On our first day in Essex some third year students had been handing out questionnaire papers in the lecture hall. I couldn't keep my eyes off mini-skirted Belinda Fluffy with her perfect face and figure. I used to see her around but didn't think a new boy like me stood a chance with her. Halfway through the year in the Easter term we were both in need of a change. She'd just been chucked by her boy friend and I needed to focus on my studies. She was an artist at oral sex but couldn't have a 'normal' orgasm. She was hard-working, neat and tidy and we needed each other. I moved into her study bedroom, making a double bed on the floor and settled into domesticity with her 3rd year pals who were all swotting for their finals.

Years later I would meet her mate Christine as librarian at University of the West of England, when I went back to college to become a teacher. One of our best laughs was lying in bed waving to the builders finishing off the next tower block. The previous year, back in Britain, I had been that builder, ogling the lasses passing by below.

The normality factor worked for a while but the political clock was going out of control, it was 1968 and that summer term the whole university was on strike. Students fought police during a demo over some visiting speakers from the government's chemical warfare establishment at Porton Down. Three students were suspended. It was in the national newspapers. We had a sit-in to get them re-instated. The London School of Economics and other universities had sit-ins for other reasons and the first demos against the Vietnam war were happening.

Belinda had finished her exams and gone home, normality had diffused. I met a nice Swedish girl at a heady political demo at the LSE. Students in Paris were rioting. The whole country came out against de Gaulle – he had passed his sell-by date – it was 23 years after the 2nd World War. My exam prospects were sliding. I had loads of unfinished work. Our Economics lecturer was as dry as a blotting-paper sandwich and Sociology was a theoretical snake disappearing up its own arse. Computing, Statistics were poorly taught for those that weren't naturals and poor Mrs Court, our Spanish teacher was always saying "You 'ave a good Espanish accent, Mr Goodchild, but you must a-learn your Berbs!"

I decided to go to Paris for the revolution instead on the pretext of taking photos for the university newspaper. I teamed up with Chris Ratcliffe, a donkey-jacket wearing activist, adventurer and hardliner, one of the participants in the Porton Down demo. We set off for Dover to join the revolution with what was left of our student grants! 30 years later Chris would help organise a re-union of Essex activists near the London School of Economics the week General Pinochet, ex-president of Chile was arrested in London by a socialist government.

Jackie Reuter was there, a Jewish girl I always fancied. Her ambition was to be a bored graduate housewife. She actually ended up running for her life from Pinochet's CIA-sponsored coup against a democratically elected government in 1973. She married a Chilean photographer in the aftermath. In the late 1980s she became active as a pro-Sandinista TV researcher supporting the Nicaraguan liberation struggle against American imperialism. The week of Pinochet's London arrest she had just got the job of director of the Children of the Andes Project in Colombia – some bored graduate housewife!

1968: PARIS

All of France was on strike including the boats. We had to go to Ostend in Belgium and head south. There was zero traffic. The country was shut down. What little transport there was stopped for us. The gates of 19th century factories were crowded with red flag waving workers on picket duties.

We arrived at night along Parisian streets eerily empty of the usual bustle, following the route along the Seine to the centre. As we arrived at Boulevard St Michel where it hits the river near Notre Dame island I could see all these huge black bubbles on the bridge. It was the battle-helmets of the CRS with reinforced stainless steel strips reflecting the night lights. They were gathering for their nightly skirmish, sweeping up St Michel to reclaim it from the students of the Sorbonne and their many comrades who had occupied it by day. A daily battle would ensue, the CRS working uphill firing the outlawed CS gas and baton charging small groups of the opposition. The students would pull out stones from the fan-shaped cobbles and launch them at the Police together with any CS cans they could gather. The students were dressed for battle too with leather jackets and crash helmets.

At two in the morning when it had died down the army would come by, sweep up and remove the evidence of the CS gas from the world's press. We ended up staying in the Censier, the science faculty, sleeping on the lab tops. During the day we moved around student meetings in the old Sorbonne University and helped print leaflets. A lasting image was a 2CV turning up stuffed full of lemons to combat the CS gas, its roof rolled back with a dozen armfuls of baguettes poking out. There was a fantastic feeling of solidarity all around.

The French are educated, creative and argumentative people, kept in check by the structures of the Napoleonic code and the need to rebuild after their humiliation by the Germans. The cynical move towards an unjust war against the Vietnamese provided a touch paper that was ignited by striking students at the University of Nanterre, the autocratic intransigence of de Gaulle and his right-wing government. It was time for a change and the people of France voted with their feet.

There was a genuine and common front between intellectuals, students and workers. The buzz of solidarity and common purpose pervaded the streets. Everyone was talking to one another. If you wanted to get somewhere you stuck out your thumb. Someone would skid to a halt and say "Where can I take you?" My Gran told me stories of life in the Blitz during the 2nd World War and hiding out with hundreds of others in tube stations – the sharing, caring and laughing together. There was this communal feeling in France that was going against the new politics of individualism, alienation, division of communities and the beginnings of soul-less American-style consumerism that was focusing life into the separate self rather than the common whole.

My excuse for being there as University of Essex photographer was a bit thin, particularly as I had a cheap camera, very little film and no money – as usual. On Bastille Day we made our way to the Place de la Gare de Lyon. We were stuck in a human sea. My pictures show an unbroken mass of people in four directions as far as the eye could see. We made friends with a group of science students and we were making our way through the Latin Quarter near the Sorbonne one night when there was a sudden charge of the C.R.S. from out of nowhere. We twisted and ran down cobbled streets. I can remember this hulking great guy, helmet strapped to his chin wearing a long rubberised mac, a baseball bat-size truncheon gaining on me by the foot. We ran into a doorway. It opened and a group of students dragged us in. By some miracle, without even knowing where we were, we had found the headquarters of the French National Union of Students. Roneo machines were spinning away knocking out leaflets, a cheerful group of lasses made us coffee and we stayed through the night. We had tasted the revolution.

The cash was gone and we had bunked off one week before our exams. We bungled and blundered our way back to Britain in time for me to fail my first year exams. In a funny way it did me a favour. I had nowhere to go. The previous nine months had been so volatile that I was glad to get a mindless job shifting milk in the Colchester dairy and commute through summer-ripe fields to work. My reality therapy was to place 24,000 bottles a week, ten at a time on fingers and thumbs upside down on a huge, constantly moving 20-pronged device that would deliver them into the steamer. My soft-faced partner Fred had been doing this same job for 20 years and his perma-nently hunched shoulders showed it.

The few of us that were left around formed more solid friendships and I started saving to go on holiday to visit the Swedish lass I'd met in the London School of Economics.

SUMMER 1968: SWEDEN

itch-hiking and travel was so popular in 1968 that when I got off the boat at Ostend I had to keep walking past about 40 hitch-hikers until I reached the last roundabout. I put down my bag expecting to wait for ages and stuck out my thumb. A car stopped immediately and I travelled up the heavily industrialised Soar valley into Germany, keeping going through the night. Northern Germany and Denmark were toy-town pretty and I caught the ferry to Malmo. There was the same hitch-hiker scene there, must have been 60 or more. That day Swedish TV broadcast that there was a record number of hitch-hikers in Sweden. I chose a side-road, cutting across country and got a lift with some lads in an old bull-nose Volvo. They had a red-haired, freckle-faced, absolutely gorgeous sister with them who was so beautiful I had to look the other way.

I was dumped on some sunny side road and trudged, hot and sticky through the undulating hills of the South Swedish Moraine. Another long lift dropped me at a cross-roads in an endless distance of identical fir tree forest. I walked on through an enclosing night fearful of bears and monsters. A trickle of traffic cheered me and I was beginning to feel less claustrophobic and lonely when I was picked up by a truck and then left in the middle of Sweden near Jonkoping on a stretch of brand new half-built motorway. I stood half the night in the same place until I fell over with tiredness. I found a builders' open-sided shed and lolled on my rucksack until first light. Glittering lakes and distant buildings emerged from the dark. I walked along unfinished debris-bordered traffic lanes and suddenly found a very old discarded bike. I pulled it out of the dirt, righted it and wobbled a couple of miles downhill to an open service station by a lake. I was carrying a very small amount of dope in my pocket and I nearly fell over again when a couple of fur-hatted cops pulled up in a car and rolled down the window.

"How did they know?" I thought, in a paranoid fluster. The nearest, bearded, one looked at me and said in English.

"You have taken the bicycle. We do not do this in Sweden. Thank you. You must take it back." What a relief. I pushed it back a few hundred yards and dumped it. Talk about a Big Brother state. It wasn't even six in the morning and someone had grassed me up. Still, stealing bicycles is about on the same level as stealing from churches but I still reckon it was dumped or used by the road workers to go for a piss.

A lovely old couple in an old Volvo version of a Morris Traveller picked me up soon after and took me for a slap-up, healthy Scandinavian breakfast. Stockholm was big, bustling and tidy. I found Birgitte's flat at 4 Berger Jallsgaten and met the Mum, Dad and enchanting eight-year-old sister. Birgitte was working so I spent all day mooching about Stockholm, which was boring and expensive. Down town there was a plaza with big curved walls where anyone would write what they liked. A team of guys would come every night and paint it all clean. Cigarette paper were more expensive than dope and the parks were full of red-faced alcoholics. The strict drinking laws with government off-licences means that the Swedes are the greatest home-brewers in the world. Years later I stayed with some builders. The litre bottle of vodka we took vanished in minutes and out came the tomato vodka from their broom-cupboard still. Early next morning after a most-of-the-night drinking session they pulled on insulated carpenters' overalls and stuffed their nail belts full of more cans, like bandoliers of beer. It gives me a hangover just thinking about it.

Birgitte and I managed to fit in lunch time sex sessions but I was beginning to experience that unbearable lightness of being that gave Sweden's perfect social system the highest suicide rate in Europe. Her father was an inventor who worked for the Swedish Ministry of Defence. Sandwiched between Russia and NATO, there was a line of airfields up the spine of the country. He had to go and inspect them and took me with him. I got dropped off in funky little towns for a couple of hours while he checked radar sites. We travelled through the long summer days to the far north where huge lorry loads of timber and iron once lumbered towards Russia in ungainly looking Soviet trucks. It was my first sight of the Russky menace that perpetuated thirty years of expensive war games for the privileged officer classes of all concerned and trillions for the arms industry. Meanwhile the defeated Germans and Japanese were getting on with inventing really useful things that would keep us busy in times of peace like comfy cars, playstations and walkmen.

Weekends we spent at their summer house in the lakelands of Uppsala, all honey-coloured logs. In the kitchen a pole of circular Rye

Vitas with holes in the middle hung drying over our heads. Birgitte and I would invent new ways of furtive fondling and rowed out one morning to a semi-submerged old wooden trawler. I actually got on best with her little sister and we would spend hours fruitlessly trying to spear fish or making toy boats. The days were shortening and it was time to hitch south and say bye to the rye bread breakfasts and my kind hosts.

In Paris with my last cash I bought a bottle of wine, a round of Camembert and a stick of bread and headed for the station to blag the train home. By one of those continuously occurring coincidences I met one of my leftwing, socialist-comrade, Essex lecturers and his girl friend getting on the train and he stood me the fare back home

BROKEN AND BUSTED

I'd had a healthy pan European summer, seen something of other cultures and was ready to get stuck in to my studies and make something of my life. I went to spend a week in Brighton painting houses to gather up some cash before heading back to our rustic student house in Wivenhoe. The last evening I worked late white-washing a wall in the last of the day's bright light. Finishing as twilight fell I jumped on my scooter and flew down Sackville Road, indicating right at the lights. Throttling down my accelerator cable broke. The engine roared at full revs and in the confusion I completed the turn right at the lights manœuvre. My unadjusted, staring at white walls eyesight didn't see the grey-green Hillman Hunter coming the other way. It hit me broadside on and I spun straight over the roof, smacking both ankles as I went and ending up crumpled in the gutter. If I had been driving a motor cycle I'd have been dead. I stood up wonkily, walked across the pavement, looked blearily at a couple of people who had rushed to my aid and said "I feel tired, I'm going to lie down." and curled up next to a garden wall in a fœtal ball.

I woke up in an ambulance with somebody cutting my favourite fawn Chelsea boot off a limp-looking foot. Thank goodness for the National Health Service. With my lovely scooter wrecked and two knackered feet I decided to head "home" to my dysfunctional pals at Wivenhoe. I lurched on trains, crossed London by tube and made it to Wivenhoe station. Carrying my pannier box full of clobber and a rucksack on my back I hobbled home looking forward to a spliff after the rigours of the journey. I had a Cigarillo box with a quarter ounce of hash in it marked out in quid deals, not so much to deal but to finance my own smoking. Anyway, it only cost £8-£12 for an ounce of the best 'Paki black'. I passed the front windows of the cottage, grateful that someone was in. A man in a sports jacket was standing in the front room. Funny, I thought, must be the landlady's boyfriend. I shuffled round to the back door and leant my weary weight on the wall via my pannier box.

Some uncanny instinct made me reach into my pocket, pull out the Cigarillo packet and hold it under the box. The unknown man answered the door. "Hello, d'you live here?" Over his shoulder I could see my mate Dane with his long red locks and black felt cowboy hat. "Hey, Paul, we've been busted!" Mr Nice turned into Mr Nasty. "Shut up, you," he snarled as the tiny upstairs door opened and four over sized bobbies emerged from the tiny, twisting stairs, knocking their heads on the roof as I dropped my narcotic packet neatly between a carpet of wide nasturtium leaves.

It was Essex University's first dope bust. They had barged into John Dunningham's bedroom where he was ensconced with his girl-friend reading a Marvel comic.

"All right! Where is it?"

"What?"

"The hashish."

"Oh, on the mantelpiece in a jar." John was and is a lovely bloke, one of the original good vibe tribe dope dealers and smugglers that did it for fun and to turn people on rather than purely for the cash. His Dad was a squadron leader in the RAF, 2nd World War fighter pilot, subsequently a V bomber commander with his finger on the nuclear button. It did not do John any good. He got 15 months in prison. We were all carted off to Clacton clink. I jabbered incessantly about the injustice of their breaking up our home and in particular holding innocent little me just out of hospital. Our village policeman eventually drove me home. He was not much older than us, a pleasant-faced fellow who never threw his weight about. He was apologetic.

"I haven't got anything against you people. I much prefer your lot compared to the drunks I have to pull out of shop windows every Saturday night."

Years later I would smoke dope with ex CID Sergeant Jim of the first Bristol drug squad.

"I left my job when I got fed up working with the bad guys and busting the good guys." The dope business has changed and so have the drugs. Now it's mostly a violent criminal activity with dealers hanging about outside schools where ice cream vans used to rule.

Our happy home of hippies was destroyed by the boys in blue. The sense of summer stability had been speared by a spiteful September fright. However, things were going to get better before they got a hell of a lot worse.

The previous year's student shenanigens caused most of the students offered places to accept. Essex was seen as one of the most radical universities in the country. Stuck in the cultural vacuum of

Colchester we had no option but to go loco. The University had made a statistical calculation that a certain percentage would take up places elsewhere. So much for Statistics! Good old Professor Lipsey's *Positive Economics* slogan was *ceritus paribus* – this or that will happen if all else remains equal – well, that's a nonsense in a rapidly changing world. Similarly, if the great non-science of Sociology had any truth then, given the amount of money that's been spent on university courses, research etc. and all the incomprehensible books disguised as so-called objectivity in the last thirty years, then why haven't we got a perfect society by now?

It is precisely because conditions change as you observe them. It is only the poets and the Divine who can define the universal truths that run through mankind's experience.

One of the advantages of this welter of students was that they were all serious or wannabe serious radicals. We were the first wave of post-adolescent changelings in a new generation of universities. It was that unique formula of individuals re-forming their adolescent identities and a set of purpose-built institutions to do it in engineered by the socialist/idealists of the previous generation and it was totally free!! No wonder it was going to get silly! Joking apart, the universities were there to educate the élite of tomorrow's concrete-and-glass nirvana. The problem was, that during that heady summer a universal adolescent energy boiled over into revolt against the old order right across Europe, America and South America. Social pundits, historians, journalists like Aaronovitch and his overpaid pals can look back and sneer at the futile attempts at "revolutionary rhetoric". The truth is that a "cultural" revolution started there and then that has affected mainstream life in so many ways that are taken for granted in the mad rush of humanity.

Music went from the single "Star" to the "Group" of mates and has passed full circle, tied itself into infinite contortions until it's arrived back as pre-packaged boy/girl bands and thumping all-night techno played by a robot on ketamine. Along the path miracles have occurred. The vegetarian, organic, wholefood business grew from student muesli roots. Stand-up comedy, rustic ruin renovation, recy-cling, resurgent arts and crafts, back to the garden communities, the mind-boggling galaxy of class 'A' drug consumption from mild mescalito revelations to crackhead criminals, dead soul junkies and the new church of the ecstatic trance dance generation. From bombs in politicians' dustbins to dead comrades and the disappeared of South America.

We went from Getting Married to the first birth control pills and the "partner" and then all the somersaults of sexuality in and out and all around. Who would have thought that 2 million peace protestors would queue to get into Hyde Park in February 2003 and in July and same year 80,000 gays from all over Europe would arrive in the same place for the Gay Mardi Gras. Pity about the rain. All of this is a 30 year timespan!

As an élite student class we had worked really hard to get halfway up the mountain of progress and been admitted to the exclusive cable car club for a ride to the top from whence illumination would guide our downhill path – pity the entire mountain range got moved on the way.

The university was full of bright-brained people up for a change. One of the advantages was that there was a plethora of handsome lasses – the Languages/ Literature/ Social Sciences faculties were bigger than Maths/ Science and the new subjects, Sociology, Anthropology, Politics seemed to attract more lasses than lads. Being an old timer with a bit of a reputation – busted and on the front line of the French Revolution with "working class" credentials, I started to become Mr Popular with the girls. I don't know whether I was stoned or just lazy but I immediately hit it off with a bunch of girls in Flat 1 of Raliegh Tower, that way I didn't have to climb the stairs.

Jackie Gallard and Vain Dipschitz soon became lovers and it got complicated. Jackie was, and is, a soul sister, smothered in makeup and draped in black velvets and red, she was an early proto-punk/ Goth although she insists she was just being a Biba girl. A genuine intellectual who devoured books and hated intellectuals, she had worked with Henry Williamson on *Tarka the Otter* and could quote Oscar Wilde. She was from the Oval with four sisters and three brothers and spoke with a genuine Saaf London accent. Handsome, curvy, bigger-hearted, she was an instant mate. Vain Dipschits was a soul seller. Hampstead Jewish big-eyed emptyish and pretty, she knew how to pull strings and unluckily for me fell in love with me there and then.

Jackie's wit and joie de vivre were too big for me and she was in love with me too. By one of those recurring coincidences, it turned out that her grandmother knew mine and I can remember meeting this lady with her little granddaughter on Belgrave Road, Victoria aged about three. Afterwards I ventured all the way around the corner into Warwick Way looking up at the balconies to see if I could find her. Jackie Gallard was the first lass I ever chased in my life. Don't ask me why we didn't settle down with a nice, normal lifelong relationship – we were two similar souls on the frontiers of change. We were 'students', educated, fairly street-wise, passingly talented. Our job was to explore, experiment at the edge of the new epoch, pursue the new gods of sex 'n drugs 'n revolution etc. etc. and make a lot of mistakes. I eventually introduced Jackie to the two fathers of her children.

I was able to escape the mayhem of the concrete jungle and get back to funky Wivenhoe. Lots of my mates were now starting to rent country cottages in Dedham or on the way to Clacton. Everyone was putting on parties, 'crashing' on floors and occasionally getting 'laid', as the Americans said.

VIETNAM DEMO

My career as a misfit really took off after the March 1968 anti-Vietnam War demonstrations. We were having lots of meetings about the cause but the crunch came when we rented a bunch of buses to join the protest in London. Johnny Dunningham hitched a ride to score some dope. I was wearing an old fold-out top hat I'd found in a junk shop. Loads of other universities and contingents from the trade unions, tough-looking printers, good-humoured miners, had turned out. Some of our socialist activist mates had connections with organisations or friends in other universities. Oxford Street was packed out, the same as the Place de la Gare de Lyon, Paris would be in May that year.

In the midst of this shuffling, chanting throng – "Hey, hey, LBJ! How many kids did you kill today?" – a group of policemen off to our left shouted, "Get that one in the top hat!" and I got grabbed by the shoulders and arms by two of them. A group of my mates led by Stuart Allerton, a charismatic bearded true left wing idealist pulled me free and I burrowed off through the crowd. There were just too many of us to intimidate. (Stuart, lovely man, was killed on his motorbike a couple of years later. There were a lot of us at his funeral.)

We surged in a slow trudge of funeral humanity into Grosvenor Square, ranting at the American Embassy and spilling over into the locked Square Gardens in front of it. The first row of demonstrators was forcing the Police backwards. Placards, tomatoes, bottles were getting thrown. It's funny how the shallow-stepped concrete block-house architecture resembled Essex University. I had collared one end of the Essex Banner and was hollering myself hoarse. Suddenly the Police attacked with truncheons. We might have had big mouths but most of us were babies and we ended up being dispersed. Our day of solidarity had made its mark on us as participants and thousands of others whose heads had been turned by the events and their broadcast on the news media.

The following year I was at a quietish party in Hampstead. The next door neighbours rented their house to the American Embassy – one of them was a marine. He had been on duty that day. "We had our weapons cocked and orders to open fire as soon as you came through those doors," he said. Not long afterwards panicking National Guardsmen would shoot and kill their own country folk at

Kent State University during a peaceful protest against the war. A lasting image of the times was stoned-out hippy chicks poking flowers down the barrels of Guardsmen's guns on American university campuses.

Later, in October 1968 I was in Colchester trying to be normal and do some shopping to eat some food, to do some work, when there was a noisy demonstration from a combination of university Marxists and pacifists. I didn't particularly agree with the demo. I thought it a demo for its own sake and couldn't see it radicalising the people of Colchester. I was coming out of the shopping precinct as the demo passed the Police station. I was literally waiting to cross the road. A mild-mannered, bespectacled student called Piers was carrying a placard and passing my side of the pedestrian safety barriers by a Pelican crossing. Behind, a row of policemen were guarding their entrance. All of a sudden my mate was slapped in the face by a leather-gloved hand, knocking his glasses off, grabbed round the neck and dragged along the fence towards the Police station entrance. I saw red, dropped my shopping and ran over shouting, "You fucking fascists, let go of him!" I didn't get very far before a leather-gloved hand smacked me in the face and I found myself being dragged into the Police station screaming, "You fascist swine ..." Once inside niceties were dispensed with and I got dragged down a corridor by my feet and stuffed bleeding from my scuffed backbone into a cell.

Thirty years later at our Essex re-union somebody was giving a speech and said, "One of my favourite memories from the 60s is this:" He pulled a newspaper report of my arrest. "FASCIST SWINE COLCHESTER" or words to that effect, and gave it to a red-faced me. We were released later. Some of us got a very nice looking lady brief with long fawn boots. I remember being invited to her pad in Chelsea. Another one of these evenings where in awe of the surroundings I'm sure I talked myself out of some interesting sex. When it came to the trial I had such a good case as a non-participant in the demo that I could have walked away. However, after an emotive defence by my lawyer I was found guilty of insulting behaviour. My Police escort whispered, "You were getting away with it, son, until she opened her mouth." Fined £20 – the beginning of my criminal career.

Later that year I would get done for shoplifting a steak from Sainsbury's on a midweek afternoon wearing a leather overcoat and a bowler hat!!

CHARISMA

With my war wounds from the peace demo I was about to become an Essex University peace hero. The transition from head choir boy, house captain, captain of the cross-country and cricket teams to a dope-smoking, Jimi Hendrix fan with three girlfriends who had twice been pinched by the coppers had been unplanned and swift. There's this thing called charisma that no one ever teaches you about and no TV programme does a series on, but some people are born with it. Kennedy had it by the jugload, Blair's got it – even Bush has it – pity about the brains. It is often confused with sexuality, which is easy because most charismatic people at least stand out in the crowd and, once given the chance to exercise their charisma, are powerful and apparently power is sexy.

Due to the many slaps, slapdowns and plain old disasters that I have had occur to me, I have never had a very high opinion of myself or my abilities. Leaving the institutionalised world of Royal Wanstead was a shock. A secondary modern boarding school run on public school lines ?! Public enemies number one and two to socialist engineers; a contradiction in terms with all of the disadvantages of both, ie, a crap education and the mental strait jacket of an archaic all boys' institution. There was no community of kids, mates or street culture to fall back on, nor was there any of the advantages of the "old boy" public school network to smooth the path. The exam failures had undermined my confidence and I was justifiably mesmerised by the bright spark alumni of the University of Essex.

A small example – the computer centre was brand new. I did a tiny bit of Statistics and Computing when I could untangle myself from long-distance liaisons in time, or find my way through the purple haze. It didn't turn on my lights at all. One day I was walking through the square and I found a computer punch card, the type we had used for our university applications.

"Cripes!" thinks I. This must be important – I turned it over and on the back it had printed out "Fuck this for a lark!"

Anyway, life was **hot** at Essex. It was still 1968. We had some of the most radical professors, lecturers and students in the country. A large official meeting of the Students' Union was called to debate the Vietnam war, the Police bust-of the demo and other student demands.

During the debate one speaker, Keith Ives, who must have been William Hague's cousin or something, was droning on about extremism and political violence. I jumped up uninvited in front of maybe 800-900 people and said, in a voice that seemed to come from out of space, "Enough of this crap! This is what political violence is, pulled up my shirt and displayed the 8 inch graze to my spine. I waffled on with some fiery rhetoric, and the place was in an uproar. Having taught in dozens of schools and rapped to thousands of people around the planet, I can recognise that look in a crowd of faces that says "I am listening to every word you're saying."

My mate Martin reckons I could walk into a room and talk drivel and people would still lap it up – he's right. I've done it hundreds of times!! In that moment I had become Captain Charisma, Student Revolutionary.

A pair of *Sunday Times* reporters approached me and asked me if they could interview me and do some quotes. In a clear moment of self-preservation I said, "You can stick your paper up your arse!" The following Sunday a rogues gallery of student leaders appeared, including Raphie Halberstadt, Karl Marx lookalike in a yellow plastic cap and the nasty unsmiling David Triesman, later General Secretary to the Labour Party, and now Lord. Ha! Ha! As well as having a good cluster of male mates, the girls couldn't get enough of me. I wasn't complaining.

I have always been a lonely guy and the company of women is a gift from the heavens as far as I am concerned. It took me a long, long time to find out a) women are more intelligent than men in their early years b) they think differently c) despite all the bollocks about equality they are pretty obviously different from us blokes! No details, but suffice it to say I was hopping in and out of beds like a rampant bunny in springtime.

The student grant was running out. I was nominally living with Vain Dipschitz in the Uni. but I didn't actually live anywhere. I was still writing to and seeing my Mum. Her comment was "They're brainwashing you up there, my son." The other homes with Dad and Uncle Peter were gone and I was getting confused about who and where I was. My personal tutor, bless him, was our Sociology Professor Peter Townshend, chairman of the Fabian Society. He took me in hand and made me write a couple of major essays for him. I produced the two best pieces of work ever for him but I was losing the plot and some nice pieces of pot as well. Most of my fellow 'radical' students could afford their indulgences. They had middle class homes and parents to fall back on and the academic discipline of a proper education. I had neither.

The bed-hopping emotional confusion, the lack of cash, the skyrocketing social changes were too much for my poor little brain. Our four ivory towers of 14-storey black engineering brick on the edge of Essex marshes, ringed with the debris of spliffs and used condoms had become a nightmare of illusion and disillusion. I was lost and sinking fast. In a moment of clarity I walked across the square one day and said to myself, "I just want to be a carpenter, married with 2.4 kids!" That's funny because that's just what I became but it took another 12 years to get there except that the statistics were slightly out.

At exactly the mid-point in my university course, half way through my second year I packed my bags and left. I'd had enough. I was going to flunk the exams again. I had no physical or emotional security and although I knew what I didn't believe in I had yet to find out what I did believe in. It wasn't going to come out of a load of Sociology text books, student sit-ins or smoking chillums – I needed some reality therapy.

1969: LUTON - STREET WITH NO NAME

Luton was real enough, a mini market town just beyond the outer ring of London, it had been clobbered by post-war industrial expansion and government housing schemes. From the M1 motorway it looked as if it had been dropped there by a massive crane. The concrete and glass functionality of Essex University was positively æsthetic compared to the overall ugliness of Luton.

It was home to two major industries, Vauxhall Motors aka General Motors Corporation of America and Luton airport, one of the sites of the burgeoning summer sun-seeker industry. I would end up working at both of them. My two best mates from school, Mick Hammond and "Stringbean" Turner were living in a 14 roomed Victorian ex-orphanage at 4 Victoria Street in the Old Town – a flyover went straight past the first floor window. They were doing Geography degrees at Luton College of Technology. Its only claim to fame was that Ian Dury, of "Sex and Drugs and Rock and Roll" fame, once taught art there. Rooms were £1 a week so I moved in. It was full of lads with a single visiting female at weekends. Mick was building a 500cc motorbike in the bedroom and String was agony aunt to the lost souls – he was so good at it that he re-christened himself "Maturner"! Today he is a full-on counsellor at a junkie rehab centre.

I needed money so coming from a generation that looked on the dole as a last resort I started looking for work. All fingers pointed uphill to the Vauxhalls. I got an appointment to be a trainee welder and hiked up through miles of identical red brick mega-sheds to find the body shop. Inside there was a cacophony of banging, air-bolting spot-welding and metal-cutting A never-ending, never-stopping production line of silver body shells wove in and out of booths getting bits bolted, welded on backed by a light show of arc-welder sparks. Cheerful bunches of blokes beavered away and shouted directions. I found an office above the track, met the charge-hand who took me upstairs. I got an instant nod to start the following Monday. Little did they know I was a useless student.

Getting to work was an expedition. I had barely done it for two years. Vauxhalls had some deal with the bus company that got everyone there 20 minutes early, or with one minute to spare. I have always been of the notion that if you are being paid by the hour then why get there early, particularly if, like me, you are no good at getting out of bed? I had gone from the world of liberal free choice to clocking on and clocking off every day. I chose the one minute to 8 option, which entailed a lot of running and I was quite good at missing the bus and doing even more running uphill to the factory.

My job was drilling the holes and cutting out the space in the body shell for the gearbox. I would have to get hold of the appropriate jig for the model of car, grab an air drill, whack it in place, drill four holes, turn back, grab the cutting torch and cut a 4" by 6" hole. All of this was done on the move in the body shell without doors. In the next booth, proper welders were fusing on body panels. They were all Jamaicans who were hard grafters, always sharing a laugh. They came up every day in a van from London. I would often get in a tangle and my job would run through the flap doors and they would shout, "Leave it, man. Give me de torch."

Winston was a bit of a loner and he would sometimes sit and drink tea with me. One day I was blathering on about jazz music and smoking dope. "You white guys always going on about turnin' on. Turnin' on for me is stripping a woman naked in my room."

Saturday I would get welding lessons on the Viva van line, which was tiny compared to the car line. I would get left on my own after a brief intro to the equipment and would end up making weird sculptures of cast-off components, bubbling with melted metal dribbles from my bad welding.

I got put on the production line for a short time trying to weld window columns on a moving target – yes, nice and easy. Hold the tiny welding gun in this massive leather gauntlet. Flick down the completely opaque visor. Strike the moving target of the car with the electric arc. At this point, supposedly, all is revealed through the visor and a neat line of weld is executed. Ha, ha, very funny. First off, once the visor drops you are totally blind, second, if you try to strike and miss you've just burnt a hole in the car, thirdly, by the time you've lifted the visor, tried again and missed it's too late and your welding cable's starting to get tangled up with the next guy's job.

I was posted back to hole-cutting and drilling. Luckily for me the automatic models had just been introduced so sometimes there was a long run of no work. I started to take books to work and ended up reading more books on the production line than I had at university, with my Jamaican mates rescuing me when I got carried away and the cars went floating by like missed boats, beyond the reach of my air tools.

We've all had cars that rusted away in front of our eyes. The need to keep those production lines going is absolute, so built-in obsolescence is as necessary to the life of a factory as blood is to a body. Why make a perfect product if it's going to put you out of work? The metal was so thin that we often used to punch dents in it as the cars went by. It was only the expertise of the spray booth boys that hardened the body shell with layers of paint.

Once, a car came off the track not far from me and the entire production line stopped, maybe 5,000 men. I went over to help put the car back on but the charge-hand said, "Hold on, mate, that's not your job." It wasn't anyone's job and the union boys downed tools. Forty minutes later a flustered-looking, managing director came over with a team of his office staff and wrestled the car back onto the line. Imagine X thousand workers times 50 minutes of lost production.

This insight into the politics of mass production, "the line must never stop," was reinforced for me later when I landed on the North African coast and started hitching east along the solitary highway. The vast continent of Saharan sand stretching into endless distances and there was no way the Third World nomads, shanty town survivalists or dirt poor farmers were going to be signing up for an HP agreement. Production was outstripping the credit line.

There were mostly French, some Japanese and German cars. Once Europe was full up where were they going to send all these cars? There wasn't room enough or income enough to support the constant production of motors by the factories of Northern Europe. The beginning of the end of the British motor industry was already in sight.

I had taken to seeing Vain Dipshitz again, who apparently couldn't live without me. She too had dropped out of Essex and on my advice was re-applying for the more "normal" but trendy Sussex University. She was living at home in Hampstead with her Jewish parents. I would hitch down to see her two or three times a week, go for a meal or to the cinema and enjoy lovey-dovey embraces in her tiny bedroom before hitching back through the night to Luton.

On one of these trips I was picked up by a private pilot who flew 6-seaters out of Luton. He was a sound, friendly guy and reminded me of my own dream of being a pilot. Back at the orphanage, the lads

I had turned on to hashish the summer before had turned into acid heads and were becoming proselytisers of the new religion of the third eye. Our house was becoming hipsville of Luton town. The music was blasting out, the clothes were defining their own fashion.

Womenfolk appeared. Mick's life-long partner Carole moved in. Rod "The Crook" Groom, ex-military policeman and criminal heavy arrived with girlfriend Marie-Anne and told us all about the tales of Lobsang Rampa. Marie-Anne would later take a fancy to String and they would have two kids. A couple of girls moved in for a short while, one a runaway half-Italian lass, mother of three. We had mother/lover sex that made my toes tingle. The following year I got a letter saying she wanted to see me to talk about something but I was already gone in more ways than one. Was this bambino no.1 for me?

A guy called Liam, an Irish ex-builder and croupier moved into the basement**. He was recovering from divorce and a spell in the nut house. He'd never smoked dope or come across hippies but he lapped it up, sitting in his room playing Cream or Hendrix. He would later become the father of Jackie Gallard's first child, Dominique. My fault, as I introduced them. We were getting off our heads on good acid and giving away free orange juice under the flyover and I had started writing poetry on and off the wall. A second summer of love had arrived and it was time for me to get out the travelling bags.

** *Years later I was passing by on the flyover at first floor window level. Vicky Street was being demolished. A single basement wall stood where Liam's bed had been. "In the White Room With No Curtains", a line from Cream, was written in foot-high letters by Liam's stoned hand.*

Amazingly, later still, in 2005, I was in Hebden Bridge editing this book with Chris Ratcliffe, from Paris 1968, who had become my publisher. I was staying with another old Essex-scene chum, Kevin Crumb the under-neighbour on the hill. He had lived for years with Jill Barron ex-girlfriend of Pete Brown who wrote most of the lyrics for Cream.

"White Room" was actually written for her. Smaller and smaller world!

1969: IBIZA – FEAR OF FLYING

I had studied a bit of Spanish at Uni., read *Homage to Catalonia* by George Orwell and as a full-on Sagittarian, with Sagittarius rising I am happiest heading for the horizon. I had done a two-week camping stint on the Costa Brava in my first year with Linda Woolley so I was ready to go further. Morocco was the target. I was hitching down to London a couple of weeks before leaving when I got picked up by my pal the pilot.

"What are you up to now?"

"Oh, I'm going to Spain."

"Well, why don't you take a lift with me? I'm flying to Geneva next week."

"... er, thanks."

Despite wanting to be a pilot I had never flown before, but I arranged to be at Luton airport at eight o'clock in the morning a week hence. Given the stranglehold Vauxhalls had on the bus timetables and the fact that Luton was a charter-only airport, there was no way I was going to get there for eight o'clock. The only way to do it was to stay there overnight. I overpacked my rucksack and got on a late bus. I dozed on and off through the night, waking myself up in a paranoid sweat every so often, thinking I was late. Eventually, in a bleary-eyed state I met Don and his two passengers.

We walked out onto the runway and boarded a twin-engined Cessna. I was stuffed in the back with my pack and we taxied down the runway. I felt a little like a fly on my own shoulder, not quite there. The strips of concrete apron sped by faster, but not that fast and we bumped up and down like riding pillion on a motor scooter and with a mild stomach-dropping sensation we were airborne and lifting up over Greytownsville and green English fields to a perfect blue Channel with yellow coast snaking north.

I eagerly explored the Geography until my eyelids drooped in mid-Channel and fell into a deep untroubled sleep. I awoke with a violent jerk. The windscreen was full of rolling black fog and the aircraft was tossed on currents of air. It was just like one of those 'B' movies with the old Dakota pitching around in a rolling studio fog, just before it hits the mountain! I didn't have time to be petrified because the next instant the clouds opened to a perfect blue sky over

91

the azure snow-mountain-ringed pool of Lake Geneva. We circled in a lazy arc and touched down with a friendly bump.

The airport was even smaller than Luton and we passed through without showing passports. I said a dazed "Goodbye and thank you," to Don, walked outside and stuck my thumb out. A carload of young people pulled up immediately and I was rolling down steep-sided mountain passes towards France still half asleep. I reached Barcelona the second day and headed for a campsite. I was the sole inhabitant apart from a hundred thousand giant ants. The full loneliness of my situation hit me. I had dropped out of the university I had worked so hard to get to, left behind all my new and old mates and was on the frontier of the unknown. I checked my map and noticed an island not far off the coast called Ibiza and thought, "OK, Morocco is too far, why not branch off to Ibiza." Two ferry lines were marked, one from Barcelona, the other from Valencia.

I had already had enough of Barcelona, so I headed south, still feeling sad and lonesome. It was a struggle of a day passing into night. I didn't fancy another lonely night in my tent so I kept going. After a long boring wait a tiny Fiat 500 pulled up with two girls in the front and two boys in the back with the rolling roof pulled open. They were en route to a student conference in Valencia, spoke a little English and swopped songs as we bumped through the night. It was one of a handfull of absolutely memorable hitch-hiking rides and the point at which I was bewitched by Spain. What did it was the smell of orange blossom in the air from the ranks of best Valenciano orange groves we were passing through. The Spanish word for the scent of orange blossom is 'azahar', derived from the Arabic and years later I wrote this poem that has always stuck with me as personifying that particular taste of Spain that has intoxicated so many different types of North Europeans.

A lonely boy in a foreign car
with the scent of
orange blossom in his nose
looking for a Spanish rose

We stayed together that night in a pension in old Valencia and I again experienced that sense of community and inclusiveness that sets the Spanish apart from other European races. Maybe it was that shared inheritance and cameraderie of war and suffering at the hands of Franco and his mobster pals; what I call the "unquenchable mercury of mankind's intelligence" that had survived and created an alternative mentality.

The next morning I discovered the delights of the Spanish market place with giant strawberries, monster lettuces and a profusion of peppers, fruits, onions, legions of strange fish and squid. I stopped and bought boots of real yellow Spanish leather that had car tyre soles and were strapped at the back. They were five pounds and the best footwear I ever had.

Years later, after having been a leather worker myself, I made a trip to Valverde del Camino, home of the Spanish leather trade, over towards Extramadura. My Valenciano boots had been called Botas Carteras; Postman's boots and I was looking for the makers. Valverde is full of houses with large entradas stacked with different kinds of footwear. Each family specialises in a particular style, traditional cowboy boots or one-off 'Elvis Presley' specials, sandals, ladies' high heels and at last Botas Carteras – they didn't have my size but I bought some for the kids. It was a bootmaker's pilgrimage, looking for the source of another taste of Spain.

1969: VALENCIA – IBIZA

The Ibiza boat out of Valencia was small and packed with travellers, mostly Spanish. Returning islanders had boxes of goods, vegetables, fruits, chickens and even a goat. Rolling dolphins played escort in the waves. I met assorted other lost souls and as we chatted the journey through, surrounded by mellow Mediterranean blue, the gold-brown rocky shoreline of Ibiza appeared and we docked onto a single white jetty with ranks of tiny houses creeping up the hillside of Ibiza town.

Myself and a couple of fellow travellers found a pension and congregated around a hole-in-the-wall English bar. The small ramblas had a couple of bars, a shop and a bank. We went to change money and a loud cheer broke out from some French people – de Gaulle had abdicated. We all joined in the cheering. Passing back down the ramblas Jean-Paul Belmondo and Ursula Andress were having an evening cocktail. I'd swear she gave me the once-over. I teamed up with a guy called Geoff from Hounslow who was a short-back-and sides Londoner in a plain sweatshirt. He was a laid back recent escapee, a working-class lad who wanted out. His gift was fishing and I would go along with him and watch with amazement as he hooked a dozen fish out of the water from where they lay basking under the boats, waiting for tit-bits like cats in a mountain village. Meanwhile the earnest fishermen with their complicated tackle were catching nothing on the end of the pier. Geoff would surface in my life years later as the owner of a remote house in Sciathos, Greece, where my ex-girlfriend Lizzie Milner was living, a long way from Hounslow!!

Gradually a group of us formed, two nice American girl students from Paris, a Dutch dude whose Dad was big in Philips, a tough older, but friendly West Coast American, Baron le Pigeon, Geoff, myself and an English girl. We headed across to the other side of the island to San Antonio. There was a single hotel and a single bar that didn't try very hard. We found a house to rent on a promontory overlooking the sea. Geoff supplied fish and the girls cooked and we made a happy community for a couple of weeks or so. One night I went off alone to town and being slightly pissed, got lost on the way back. I came across a solitary Guardia Civil with patent leather tricorn hat, on a Lambretta. He kindly gave me a wobbly ride home to our hacienda!

Funny to think that San Antonio is now the party capital of the world and is apparently bursting with hotels, clubs and off-their-heads English kiddies. It was a very trippy kind of place before the influx of drugs, ideally summed up in the film 'More' by those increasingly comprehensible boyos the Pink Floyd.

I was well warmed by my experiences and the sense of the creative community outside of the sex and drugs and revolution scene I had left behind in England. For the first time I came across wandering poets, artists, leather workers, musicians, Vietnam deserters who were all searching, but had something to say along the way.

I had lent the American girls a small amount of money and had an invite to stay in Paris, so I started the long hitch-hike north from Ibiza via Barcelona. Anyone who has ever hitched through France will know the long existential torture of the three days stuck in Narbonne. The summer-of-love vibe had got stuck either side of Narbonne's new municipal housing blocks backed by dry limestone outcrops and rolling slopes of gorse and aromatic herbs. Right at the beginning of the ordeal, while I was hitching with a Canadian pal, two Italians in a sports car stopped. I was puzzled. They didn't have any room. The passenger walked over and said "Hey, Paul, remember me?" It was Antonio, the waiter from my Dad's hotel in Hove!! They didn't have room but it was enchanting to meet a friendly face in that inhospitable place.

I eventually trudged my way out of the Narbonne trough and got a series of short rides on the motorway network. At the end of a tired long day I came out of the service station toilet to see a Godfrey Davis rent-a-van parked in front of me. The driver looked up, bearded, Latino looking.

"London?" I said, pathetically.

"Yes, come on. I have to be quick." I jumped in, grateful to be sat on the squeaky plastic seats of a Mark 1 Ford Transit.

Dante Mairana was from Catania, Sicily. A would-be photographer he had been working on someone else's shoot and was driving the equipment to London via Orly airport in Paris. We chatted through the night. He was a truth-seeking runaway. His father was a senior psychologist in Sicily. He had just got himself a contract from a Sicilian drinks firm and asked me if I wanted to help ... wow! We stopped at Orly to deliver a package and as I stepped out of the van, there, parked just over the fence was a brand new Concorde airliner stuck up on the gangly stilts of her undercarriage, the beak of her landing cone dropping down looking for all the world like an awkward but graceful supersonic stork. Thirty years later I would be teaching in Monk's Park School, Bristol within sight of Filton ærodrome where she was made. Because I kept a group of kids behind for 4 minutes we caught sight of Concorde on her last flight and watched her circle, dip her wings over our playground and land for the last time, nose cone dipped, half a mile from us. Many of the kids' relatives had worked on the original aircraft.

Dante and I headed into Paris to find the American girls from Ibiza. I was just reading the street map, knowing that we were near when I looked up and saw one of the girls crossing in front of us – I'm not a gambling man, but what are the odds on that in a city of 5 million plus? We enjoyed a cheerful reunion and were both treated to a night between the sheets with the ladies – life was on the up again.

LONDON PHOTO PHONEYS

I was now a fully-fledged drop-out. It's a pity you can't get life skills modules to add to formal qualifications. The music was getting weirder – Kevin Ayers, and Gong were singing about 'raining golf balls in a land of pink and grey'. Dante the Sicilian photographer and I started working together. He was organising models and shoots and I was running around getting props and blagging bits and pieces from my Mum. He had a nice New Zealand wife and a basement pad in Bayswater. Another flat was rented for the shoots and I ended up staying there and being tea boy and secretary.

A couple of models turned up one day, a very blonde handsome guy and a lovely Australian lass called Ceridwen Greenfield. I was completely star-struck, of course, which is pretty stupid in retrospect, but it was all part of my post-Uni reality therapy and it beat working in a car factory for sure. Ceri and I took a liking to each other and became lovers for a while. She was staying in a Bohemian basement pad off Holland Park, very different from her model-girl image. I started hanging about Notting Hill Gate and came across a flatload of Essex/Oxford graduate students who always had wicked dope for sale. I knew one of them an ex-Essex comrade who is now a Labour MP. Having met Howard Marks and read *Mr Nice* I'm pretty sure this was a part of his early empire. It was a very paranoid experience hanging around Notting Hill in those days. Anyone with long hair was seen as an anti-social dole-scrounging stoodent narcotics abuser. You could get it in the neck from the Police just for having a packet of Rizla papers with the cardboard torn off.

It was fun working with Dante. There was bugger all money around so I took a job as a dustman in Hampstead to earn some cash. It was a healthy outdoor job and we finished at one every day. Meanwhile I met up with some other ex-Essex folks and I was staying in a flat in West Hampstead with two New Zealanders and a very far-out dope-smoking musician who used to like sitting around playing his guitar in the nude. Bryce, one of the Kiwis was famous as a folk singer in New Zealand. Trouble is he had taken a lot of acid and had written a song called Whitey the Magic Whale which had got him banned from the airwaves back home. His companion, Robin, was a theatre and radio producer and they had both come to try their luck in swinging London. I used to get them very good dope and Robin took a fancy to me for a while. She had been working in some club and one night while we were lying in bed King Freddie of Buganda and his retinue turned up and stayed for an hour or so. It was pretty obvious that he or one of his boys was after the blonde-haired Robin.

I got Bryce a job on the bins and shortly afterwards there was a well-publicised London-wide strike. It was just after a character called The Singing Postman had made it big in the charts. Bryce wrote a dustman's song and ended up on TV as The Singing Dustman.

1969: Down in Rome All Alone

The summer was closing and the sixties were running out. Dante was off to Italy to finish off his project and invited me along for the drive in his Mini Innocenti. He still owed me some money so I went along. When we arrived in Rome Dante decided it would be better if he dropped me off while he sorted things out with his uptight family in Sicily and got the money for the job which he would forward on to me. We were hanging around in Plaza Santa Maria in Trastevere, a funky square away from the centre and home to Bohemians, travellers, poets and people on the edge of the film business. Fellini was making 'Satyricon' and the Spaghetti Western genre was booming. I gladly stayed on and immediately met Patricia, the much older mother of two American leather-worker lads I had met in Ibiza. She put me up for a few days.

Walking across the square one night I met Thea Khanis, half Lebanese half Mancunian, who had been at Essex. I ended up staying a couple of nights with her in her parents' Arab-furnished penthouse flat and having breakfast of Kellogg's corn flakes with her Granny from Manchester over a formica table. Her Lebanese Dad worked for the UN. One day Thea came up to me and in her frank, open way invited me to go for guerilla training with the PLO First off, I am a coward until I get angry. Second, I was a fully flowered-up hippy living in the moment. Nice offer, but no thanks.

The Trastevere was full of characters. David, blonde-haired handsome ex-London policeman who found occasional film work for himself and others. Then there was petit, slightly bald Georgio, always dressed in black, and his red-haired mate Benino, a couple of local lads. They would always drink coffee in the corner cafe opposite the pastry shop. They took a liking to me and we went on long walks through town, them eyeing up the antique shops. I'm not sure what their caper was, but they certainly didn't go out to work. One day we were sauntering along, me wearing my slate-blue kaftan with exquisite white embroidery when we were accosted by a handsome tall older woman. She was a costume designer for the movies and was bewitched by my shirt. She invited me to stay in her studio. Her name was Boja Koja, Yugoslavian with two very different but beautiful daughters. I slept in the studio a few nights, getting woken by Ginger

Baker on the drums rainfall on the glass roof.

Another night I stayed with one of the daughters and her boyfriend at the very top of an old 10-storey apartment block. I woke up early and fumbled around the tiny kitchen, knocked on the bedroom door and asked if she would like a drink. She sat up in a bed spread with zebra stripe sheets backed by a giant mirror. A knackered looking boyfriend snoozed on. "It's OK," she said, "coffee's coming." There was a knock on the flat door. I opened it and found a waiter standing there with three steaming cappuchinos and a tray of pastries! Soon I got some work on a cowboy movie. I had been hanging about thinking I might be discovered! Not that I could act particularly but it was all kicking off in Rome that Autumn. My job was to sit in the blazing heat on a dry rock of limestone for two days covered in sticky makeup wearing a false beard. On the third day we were called into a big circus tent, filmed in the audience for about fifteen minutes and that was it – thank you and goodbye. So much for my Italian spaghetti western film career. I didn't even know the name of the movie.

15 years later I was switching channels on the TV late one night in Bristol when a good old cowboy film came up, a sort of Woolworth's version of *The Man With No Name*. It was called *Bud Spencer and the Circus of Hate/Love* (whatever) and he was escorting a circus wagon. I shouted upstairs to my son Robin, 8 years old (now 25 and an actor). He came running downstairs just in time to see the camera pan round a circus tent full of black-bearded miners with, for a split second, a blonde, bearded me – so much for fame!

Of all the people who hung about the square – a large proportion, including myself, were wannabes and poseurs, a single person stood out from the flock. A barefoot girl in a grey, rough poncho and a head of curls used to pass in front of the old church of Trastevere, with a herd of mini-dogs in tow. She was striking in her simple grace and – of another world. I was lit up by this apparition and made my feelings known one day while having morning coffee with Roberto and Benino. The next day he invited me to a meal with his friends in a nearby restaurant. It was old school, local and exclusive. I didn't have a clue what to eat so I asked for spaghetti. I was licking my lips with satisfaction when a plate of clams arrived, then artichokes, meat, more pasta. My glass was always full of a strong, sweet wine. It was a jolly evening and being penniless I was embarrassed by the hospitality. We left and met up with a couple of student types. We went up the street a bit, then round the back of some houses and up a back staircase along an old balcony into a one-roomed old style flat with a small kitchen and bathroom. It was furnished with a massive old cast-iron double bed with copious small pictures of saints and virgins and little else. It seemed like a Roman Catholic's granny flat.

Roberto pulled out some dope and hustled the students to make spliffs by emptying out and refabricating king-size cigarettes. We smoked without him or Benino having a toke and he got rid of the students. A few minutes later there was a knock at the door and dog-girl appeared. She came and sat on the bed, chatted for a few minutes with the lads in non-comprehensible Romano and they left! I was all alone with the fairy of the alleyways. My jaw was already dropping at her beauty, my tongue was tied with embarrassment and I couldn't speak more than ten words of Italian anyway. I feel inadequate even now, thinking about the situation.

We made love in the bouncy bed with grey blankets and she left in the night. I woke alone in the morning and stumbled into the kitchen. Roberto and Benino were sleeping fully clothed, head to toe on a tiny cot. I don't know whether he asked the girl or paid her, but I never saw her again. I don't know why Roberto looked after me so well, but I sent him a massive Winston Churchill cigar when I got back to England. Winnie strikes again.

I spent penniless days walking about bumping into other travellers trying to be interested in the Imperial sites. No money arrived from Dante and I never saw him again either nor was any Roman Romance happening. I was starting to feel lonely and outcast and walked along the banks of the Tiber crying quietly. Years later I would hear "Every Picture Tells a Story" by Rod Stewart. "Down in Rome I was so alone!!" Eventually I teamed up with a northern lass and we hitched it back to Paris and sneaked the train to Calais and where she got caught by the guard but being a girlie, got away with it.

Back to boring Blighty.

1969-70: Bright Town! Deepression!

I was so full of summer sun and shenanigans I had a dream of going back to Brighton and starting a head shop selling crafty clobber etc. Trouble was – no capital. Turned up at Uncle "wotcha cocker" Fred's and he knocked me back down to reality and got me a job cleaning windows with New Century Window Cleaners with a super-aimiable ex-crook called Terry. I moved into a pad in unromantic bungalowsville Peacehaven with a friend of Mick Sly's. Jackie Gallard's younger sister Viv took a fancy to me and I became her first real lover, though neither of us were in love.

She would later marry and have a child with a filthy rich American who turned them both into junkies and committed suicide in her 40s. Bless her soul.

Peacehaven was the antithesis of my Summer of Love dreams. Up before first light, watching water freeze on Brighton shop windows on dark mornings, being propositioned by lonely Jewish widows. I was so on the way down I nearly jumped off a block of flats I was cleaning on the sea front. The bollock cruncher came when we were sent to clean the pleasingly æsthetic, totally impractical windows of Basil Spence's futuristic Sussex University.

I bumped into Vain Dipschitz. She really wanted to see me and made a date. I was really lonely and miserable, outcast from the university Bohemian scene, cleaning windows, trying to hone my working class tone. I was stuck between two totally different worlds and it was the autumn cusp before winter darkness. She didn't turn up and I waited for hours on a cold November night. I found out she'd been out with Barnie Roadster of the well-known sports car making family, a Paul Goodchild lookalike, who she would later marry and divorce - surprise, surprise - on the make, on the take was her motto as long as it fitted the trend.

Years later I saw a meaningless movie she made about Polynesian women, cashing in on the media sisterhood syndrome. I went round to her flat, found her in the kitchen and asked her why she had not shown up. She told me a pack of lies and I knocked her to the floor amidst a stack of milk bottles and had to stop myself from kicking her there and then. I ran out of the house and down to the wave furious beach and cried my eyes out, salt-faced on the salty beach. It was the first and last time I ever struck a woman.

It was a mini class war. Hampstead trendy dispenses with working class boyfriend with a sneer once she's secured her new man with the right credentials. I cracked up a few days later cleaning the windows at the university. I went to work for a few more weeks, like a ghost, being carried by Terry, but had to jack it in. I left Brighton, went to see the old man managing a bar on a caravan site on the Romney Marsh. He wasn't interested. Bought me back to Brighton, found me a job and a room with a super-miserable Polish couple in Hove, who I'm sure counted the pieces of bog roll and hassled me for rent on the dot, Fridays at 6 o'clock. I'd get home from work and sit indoors eating Mars bars until I felt sick and feeling like a dying fish suffocating on a beach. It went on for a couple of months of twilit darkness and depression. I was so down I'd cross the road if I saw someone I knew. Brighton's always been a charming, glittery, hipster sort of a place but it is full of transients, cliques and a false ambience that offers a mirage of camaraderie that ends at closing time.

Mick Sly, my old pal from school, had gone up to Essex on my advice and was back visiting his Mum. He rolled me some dope, played me some music and turned my miserable mind back on.

I met up with Monica Willis, an old Essex friend of Jack's. She talked me into coming to stay at Essex. They were living in a funky farmhouse in the sticks and some of my old mates were that pleased to see me I made a pretence of trying to get back into Essex Uni. Gradually the lights started coming back

I remember LSD being part of the process, in fact I remember taking so much that it stopped working. I hadn't had any sex for about six months when I bumped into Julia, girl friend of Pete Templeton (brother of Dougal of *Venue*, Bristol, who I would meet ten years later). They were going through that "Why don't you have sex with someone else?" phase. She still remembered fancying charismatic comrade Goodchild in her first year. She took me back to her room and took her clothes off. Luckily I remembered what to do.

I got a job on a building site on the new bypass next to the Uni. We were foundation piling; in the bottom of a river, dropping 3 metre long steel cylinders from a great height and getting covered in all kinds of crap, but it was outdoor physical fitness training for cash!

Lunchtimes I would go back to the Uni. salad bar for lunch. It was the ideal reality therapy. What put the Christmas tree lights on was a fairy called Diana Ruston.

Di was a blond, husky-voiced beauty who had gone right off the deep end of the swinging 60s and had kept her Uni. studies together as well. We had arrived in the same intake. She'd been living with a crazed New Yorker called Douggie and all his pals in a squat in Regent's Park and had come back to take her exams. She took me straight into her arms and smoked the best dope. Crosby, Still and Nash had just come out and we used to listen to it loving each other. Life was suddenly perfect. Thank you lady Di! We would stay friends for lot of years.

I went to live on a houseboat with some freaks who were just back from India and spent the summer term running down to London, buying and dealing weights of dope from one of Howard Marks' pads in Islington. (I asked him years later if he knew the house. "Oh, yes. I used to have a couple of answer phones locked up in a trunk there!!") I love the image of two answerphones talking to each other.

Around this time I met Jackie's brother-in-law and he showed me how to plait leather belts. I bought some leather and started making some belts and bags. I discovered that I was actually quite good with my hands and my stuff started to sell. By the time the new intake of students arrived, some of them fresh back from India, I was a full-on hippy leather worker, ex-revolutionary living on a house boat. I was part of what had become the English East Coast scene. People were starting to listen to the Grateful Dead and Bob Marley played the Uni. but I was too stoned to get to the gig – idiot! Di turned up from California at the end of the summer with an egg of pure mescaline. She gave me some to sell and whizzed off to Saudi Arabia where her Dad was teaching the air force how to fly. The mescaline seemed to work for some, not for others and, as paranoia increased due to the antics of the Angry Brigade I buried it. A year later somebody said "Yeah, Paul, what happened to that mescaline you had?" We went and unburied it from the pebbles by Tawney Tower. It had matured, blended, whatever, but we had the entire university tripping on it for free!

A host of interesting and interested people turned up that year and I commuted between the dope den in Islington and Essex where I now knew three student generations of people, some graduates, some drop-outs. I was starting to lug a huge bag of leather and tools about with me. Everywhere I stayed somebody would want a belt, a bag, a bracelet, chokers. My skill was flourishing and I started dyeing and tooling leather as well as plaiting it. I would make my living on and off for two years and eventually send a cowboy hat to Buffalo, U.S.A. and a pair of "thongs" (my leatherworker's answer to the flip-flop) to Australia.

A lass called Maggie started a late-night veggie food bar. A craft and Indian import shop opened in Wivenhoe. *International Times* newspaper was the 'head' chronicle that kept us informed of the progress of the cultural revolution and of ways around the dope laws. A dozen dealers flourished, street theatre groups formed, bands played and disbanded, independent cinema, alternative photojour-nalism, living in communes. This English East scene was evolving from the society of students and ex-students plus people drawn to the fire, a scattering of bleary-eyed local lads, like "Hodge" and Ian Massingham. None of this was part of the curriculum plan but it was growing of its own accord, part subsidised by all those full grants by the Welfare state, which is exactly how it should be.

In the Islington dope den at Englefield Road there was Martin Smeaton, boy friend of Natasha Lane, literature student, sister of Howard Marks' future wife. He lived on the top floor of the house and had ripped out three quarters of the ceiling, leaving one quarter for his loft/bedroom. He had knocked out the stairwell partitions, built another bed for me over the staircase, taken out doors, put in arches and rough-plastered the walls with a tiny trowel, giving a Greek taverna effect that he loved so much. The kitchen table was a 6' length of white marble fireplace top flanked by 6'x9"x3" sanded down wooden joists. He would regularly drag a trolley-load of marble or a length of pitch pine from the demolition of fine old Victorian houses on the Essex Road. He was an ex-student of sculpture at the Central School of Art and Design and a genius.

Years later I would find a picture of him in the Sunday Times supplement sitting on the head of a gold (polystyrene) Inca god as prop man at the Royal Opera House! He would end up as designer/sculptor for Ridley Scott on "The Enchanted Forest". He was the only man who could do the trees. Martin's favourite person was his Grandad, old school Shropshire farm labourer who knew his roots. He told me how when he was a lad he and his Grandad were trying to solve the problem of a flooded field. Victorian fields were often drained by small bore under ground clay pipes. A hawthorn was growing down by the stream and a thirty foot dead straight root had grown up the pipes. Funny thing cultural influences.

I was criss-crossing London, leatherworking, dossing here and there in Notting Hill, Camden and Stoke Newington and staying creatively busy. Di flit back in and we flew back together, living in smart Kensington until she flit again.

London was heaving with energy. The Oz trials were on. Political agitation continued. Dockers and printers went on strike.

ANGRY BRIGADE

In the post-Essex University dysfunctional graduate drop-out/dope depression scene a number of "revolutionary" head-quarters were established. One of them was Englefield Road, Islington, Grosvenor Avenue, Stoke Newington and a flat in Stamford Hill over a Kosher Butchers! Several more were dotted around West Hampstead, Camden Town and Notting Hill. Mostly low-rent or cheap-to-buy with the inherited five grand of our middle-class cadres, they were hotbeds of revolutionary Marxist rhetoric and high-grade hashish consumption courtesy of Mr Marks and co.

Disaffected future members of the ruling class came across these cells on their way down the A10 from Cambridge University and joined forces with their comrades. Having come of age in the imperfect socialist utopia of the post-war welfare state, many were now intent on levelling the scores against the Conservative led ruling junta.

Serious inequalities and global crimes were actually still being committed by those with power and influence. 7/87, a radical theatre group of the time highlighted the fact that 87% of the wealth of this "egalitarian" nation was still owned by 7% of the population. The United States was still involved in dropping more bombs on the small nation of Vietnam than in the entire 2nd World War, on their way to killing 1.5 million of its citizens (and that does not include those maimed or traumatised, or those killed in tertiary wars amongst their neighbouring countries). Something obviously needed doing.

We were being educated as the new district oficers of the shrunken British Empire, to supervise the New Town Nirvana and High-Rise culture of the 1960s and prepare the way for supermarket chains whose economies would be larger than most countries. For a variety of reasons, based on intelligence, intuition, and the need for every new generation to invent their own reality, we weren't having any of it. We were *angry* at the deception and delusion of much of mainstream culture and the inability of the political process to have a truthful influence on the world we had inherited and which we would one day, hopefully, grow up to run.

While the sex and drugs and rock and roll was becoming a full-blown recreational distraction, this young cohort of highly intelligent post-bohemian, feminist, working-class lads and lasses, who had been encouraged to think by the ship of state, were now planning to sink it.

Being good British citizens educated to queue and not kick dogs they selected their "terrorist" targets carefully. One demonstration involved placing severed pig's heads on the steps of the American Embassy and became front page news across Europe and America. The privileged public schoolboy elite that was and still is running the Tory party were also targeted: given that their antiquated political philosophy was a load of rubbish; bombs were placed in the dustbins of certain ministers and influential figures.

The Fuzz, knowing they were losing the war on drugs by starting to deal it themselves and enjoying a bit of sex and rock and roll on the side, had to be seen to be taking these new-age Guy 'n' Gal Fawkeses seriously. Given the conspicuous appearance of these not very flower-powered communards and their propensity to live in overcrowded conditions amongst "normal" citizens, plus their habit of publishing revolutionary rhetoric in magazines and pamphlets, they were soon nicked.

The Angry Brigade had become target of the month for the newspapers and just prior to their arrest and knowing some of them such as Anna Mendelson, Hilary Creek, Jim Greenfield and Jake Prescott I had started to develop a keen sense of paranoia despite my choice of a different path. I can remember distinctly the moment when I left the "party".

There was a group of pretty but heavy (don't give them my address!) women sat in the half-built basement of Englefield Road gorging themselves on a feast of Sainsbury's food and wines obtained by means of a stolen cheque book, as was their habit. On the telly James Baldwin, the radical gay black American writer and activist was talking to someone like Parkinson. Pam Thompson, who I think might well have been the first black lesbian in London picked up a brick and threw it at the TV, shouting "You fucking sell-out!" Being a happy-go-lucky, semi-successful truth-seeker this sort of behaviour didn't add up on my revolutionary abacus. I decided it was time to seek another way of practising my ideals.

A few days later I started to notice overly obvious people sitting in cars in the street, reading newspapers. A month or so later the Angry Brigadiers were busted. Anna, Hilary, John and Jim all got 10 years for 'conspiracy to cause explosions', by way of being made an example of by the public school prefects who were running the country, despite the Angries' Judeo-Christian respect for human life and property. (Pity about the pigs.)

The subsequent evolution of genuine small 'p' political movements actually started from these explosive beginnings; outfits like the claimants' unions, the squatting movement, which later evolved into housing associations, wholefood co-ops, adventure playgrounds, local council activists etc. formed the basis of many things which are part of our society today.

Our sacrifical lambs had gone to the slaughter, but the times were definitely changing. (I met Anna many years later, just after she came out of prison still with the same light in her eyes, and looking half the age of her unincarcerated contemporaries who were beginning to look a bit jaded and worn out from their sometimes half-baked beliefs, surfeit of Sainsbury's tucker and too much sex and drugs and rock and roll.)

The revolutionaries had kicked the ball onto the pitch and the rest of us had picked it up and run with it; the counter culture that survived and influenced so much of contemporary British society was at large and kicking.

It was a heady and exciting year and on my separate path as a modern mendicant menoevering my way through the many layers of change on the cultural frontier, I heade back to the relative safety of the grey but ivory towers of Essex.

At a Uni. gig, I was lucky enough to meet Margaret Dupee, rechristened the Maglet for her habit of appearing silently round corners, big eyes sparkling. She was so lovely and I moved in with her.

She was spiritual in an unstated way, artistic, organised and could drive her Mum's car! Compared to my way-outness she did have a certain suburban outlook. Today I reckon that's probably a good balance. We were together on and off for three years. She was pregnant twice and the only reason I didn't marry her was that I wasn't ready. I still had to go and look at the world and understand it and myself before I had children. Blessing to you Maglet Dupee, wherever you may be. She had the good sense to give me the heave-ho, lying horny as a bumblebee on a Devon hillside at the end of the second Essex drop-out year. That sent me on a tumble back down that would be exacerbated by the summer exodus of students from the scene. I had been smoking a lot of drugs, doing acid until it didn't work any more and I was facing, like many youngsters today a post LSD/drugs comedown. I stayed around the gloomy campus with no fixed abode getting very cheesed off and depressed, missing the Maglet and the exercise of my own magnetism in the empty concrete cloisters.

I met another lost soul, Joanna Gibbins, a flower-powered fairy pre-Raphealite lookalike, equally depressed. We decided to hitch hike to Ireland together. I had the address of Liam Laden, a Luton pal living in Dublin. The journey wasn't easy. We seemed to bottleneck and slow to a miserable crawl as the A5 snaked its way through wet Welsh hills. Slept a night in an open-sided barn in Corwen, a town I would become very familiar with in the future as the home of the North London drop-out scene. We took a luxury breakfast in the Betws-y-Coed hotel, made another 20 miles and slept the night wrapped in a plastic sheet under a gorse bush by the Holyhead road at the entrance to Snowdonia.

1971: DUBLIN

We made it to Dublin via a well-weathered landing at Dun Laoghaire port. Ireland was different with its humble single-storey housing, bosom country green hills wrapped in semi-permanent rain. Liam was living on a council estate at Raheny on an old Guiness family estate with a lass called Jo Bermingham and her two kids, the ex of a Brighton character Tom Bermingham. He too would surface in my future. They were dealing dope and had just started a leatherwork stall in the subsequently famous Dandelion Market. We got very stoned and agreed to set to work together the next day swapping skills and designs.

We were in for a nasty surprise. Joanne and I slept on the floor on a comfy mattress and became lovers, thankful for each others' companionship. The next day I awoke in a dopey daze. Two men in light and dark grey suits were standing at the end of the bed. Half of me thought to get up and hit them. The sensible half decided to lie doggo.

'Good morning Dennis O'Mullins, Dublin drug squad.'

We were busted again.

About five of them bungled around the house while Joe jabbered at them in non-stop distraction. A red whiskey-nosed detective knocked over a lamp with his boozer's shaky hand. A piece of nice Turkish dope popped out of the base.

"Right, lads, take the place apart!"

It was useless. They had found the personal but not **the** stash. On Monday morning when they were all in court, bar me, I had to go to the bus station left luggage locker, lift two ounces out of a pungent green Genie, "you want something" cash box and then carry it over the river Liffey bridge, feeling very iffy, to the train station lock-up. My stand-out-in-the-crowd face has always made me justifiably paranoid and I was ready to drop the lot into the muddy murk of the waters below.

We lived together doing vegetarian cooking competitions, making all sorts of bags, belts, hats, kiddies' moccasins and boots down at the Dandelion Market. Liam and Jo carried on after we left Ireland and became known as the best hippy leatherworkers in Southern Ireland. Joanna and I travelled down to West Skibbereen, helped harvest seaweed from the beach, bought a load of old rotting tack and got a treasure trove of brass buckles to work with. Back in Dublin we found Mary and Cockney Steve who we knew from Essex by one of those back-street coincidences. We went to visit them in the sticks where they were living in a barrel-topped gypsy wagon.

The combined effect of the healing powers of the Emerald Isle had lifted my depression and I was beginning to formulate a lifestyle plan. I wanted to go back to London, get a job as a craft teacher in schools or start a craft school cum commune out in the country for inner city kids. It was a coalescence of all the best bits of getting out of slumsville London that had happened to me. The Uni. scene, the turning on the dropping out, learning new values. The nurture of nature, the travel, the commune, the doing your own thing, hands-on experiences. My eyes and heart were wide open. My Sociology studies told me I was on the right track. The vision is little changed today as I write these notes. I knew I would have to get some sort of job in the youth club/social sector to start it all off. My goal was clear.

We left and hitch hiked to the North to get the boat to Stranraer in Scotland. I had got a strange letter from Martin Turner. He was offering to co-operate on starting some sort of community. He was staying with his Dad in Teviothead in the Borders. I also knew Bev, a lass from London who lived in Edinburgh who was part of the Scientology sect and knew all the alternative types about on the Edinburgh scene. We arrived at her flat in Nicholson Square. Jo left to visit parents in London. Bev immediately got me an order for ten leather cowboy hats and I set to work. The Edinburgh underground scene was humming with interesting characters, groovy music and a lot of healthy hashish, probably from that naughty Mr. Nice, a lot of people seemed to live in funky cheap stone built sub-basements, the underground under the underground.

One night Bev announced she was going to stay with that previously incomprehensible bunch of musicians, The Incredible String Band – would I like to come? What a treat! The band, acolytes, roadies, wives, children, poachers lived at the 'row' in Innerliethen. The row was just that, a ten house stretch of one and a half storey workers' cottages on the crumbling but beautiful country estate owned by Peter Tennent also owner of Mustique in the Caribbean and mate of Mick Jagger and Princess Margaret. It was the ideal commune because everyone lived in separate houses but were involved in a common cause, The Incredible String Band.

I stayed on and they were magic days, up on Robin Williamson's roof wearing a jalaba, a rope down the chimney tied to a bundle of fir branches, him pulling one end and me the other. Miranda, the lovely, long Danish/Californian woman who put me up and put up with me despite my respectful infatuation, found me work with the local hunt beating pheasants (and me a vegetarian!) Joanna arrived back in Nicholson Square and then found her own place and has lived in Edinburgh for the rest of her life.

I headed south down the A49 to find Martin Turner but he had gone back to hang out at Essex. I spent an interesting couple of days with his Dad, ex Medical Officer of Health for the Gold Coast (Ghana). He was nearly eighty, fiercely independent and lived completely alone in a house miles from anywhere on the watershed between Scotland and England.

I went south to London, stayed with my Mum. She was working the Guildhall and came home with the leftovers of the Lord Mayor's pheasant one night, then steak the next. I broke my meat fast. Thanks M'lud. Pink Floyd were playing the Rainbow theatre 300 yards from my Mum's place. I rendezvoused with the Essex "lads", Dave Thornton etc and dropped some of Di's mescaline, floating in a kaleidoscopic light beam of dust particles as Roger Waters "Set the Controls for the Heart of the Sun" - now I could groove on the Pink Floyd.

Back around the Essex East coast scene a new bevy of faces were getting distracted from their studies. I met Tom Bantock, a near relative of that cad Harry Flashman, I'm certain, dark Adonis-like ex public schoolboy. His father had been a major shareholder in the Great Western Railway, but he was going to have to wait until 27 for his inheritance. He loved horses and women, hadn't a clue what being a hippy or socialism was and didn't smoke dope 'cos he couldn't fiddle people when he was stoned! We got on in a Yin/Yang on and off sort of way. He had bought a gypsy caravan and wanted me to make him 500 leather belts so he could ride around the country pretending he had made them. He had dropped out and got a job with an icy-hearted stockbroker called Kroll, buying and looking after pedigree hunter horses. He had a free cottage in Suffolk and cajoled me into staying and starting the mass production of leather belts.

1971: MILDMAY ACTION HOUSE, ISLINGTON

I was seeing the Maglet again and enjoyed living in one place, cooking all the meals. Public school Bantock didn't have a clue. Recreation was riding thoroughbreds through 14th century oak forest, Bantock bareback, me cockney cowboy in leather hat, struggling to stay on. Other times night riding on the bonnet of Kroll's Land Rover holding a shot gun while Tom chased rabbits in the headlights with his high speed lurcher snapping bunnies' necks. I was still nurturing my dream of starting a countryside-based craft centre for inner city kids. It was a case of trying to pay back some of the incredible experiences I had been having plus combining some of the social insights I had seen as a wandering self-employed sociologist – communal living, the joy of creation and craft work, travel, mixing with all kinds of people. I was acutely aware I would have to find myself a job to start gaining experience of working with kids, as a playleader or youth worker.

I went down to London to buy leather and stayed in Islington. I strolled along the Essex Road on a fine spring morning and saw a sign saying Islington Social Services. I popped in to enquire about possible jobs. I met Lynn, a harrassed-looking social worker. She explained there was a project, the Mildmay Action House, that was in need of a playleader, but that it was descending into chaos due to the local street gang smashing the place up. I agreed to go and have a look and found a group of girls smoking fags in a back room, obviously bunking off school and a few bright-eyed lads smashing something up in the garden. I was interested so I went to see the management committee at 26 Grosvenor Road, Stoke Newington. It turned out that they were an amalgam of Essex University and Cambridge dropouts, 90% women/lesbian activists and a few working class mums and I knew a couple of them from student revolutionary days. They had persuaded the council to give them the old house and a grant to run the Action House for local single mums and older kids. The trouble was they had a programmeless manifesto and the local teenage gangs were alternately using it as their bunk off/bunk-up HQ and destroying the fabric of the building.

I took the job as playleader with a reluctant nod from some of the wimmin. Lynn arranged for me to be appointed as temporary assistant social worker for £40 a week. I had gone from theoretical Sociology to hands-on social engineering via a stint as a hippy leather worker. I got Martin Smeaton involved, knocking the place into order with 6" nails. Martin Turner appeared and started taking photos and amusing the kids. Somehow we turned destruction into creation and more kids appeared. Rob the Crook, a very wide awake, dope smoking ex-burglar turned up via the Gentle Ghost handy man's agency. He was our carpenter and kept the kids busy. He was an ex-dysfunctional kid who had ended up in Dartmoor. A month prior to release he had been sent for re-integration and group therapy sessions in Pentonville Prison. He had taken a shine to the group psychologist, Anna and proposed to meet her at Oxford Circus tube on his release. They moved in together in her long semi-circular windowed pad in Hampstead. He was now treading the straight and narrow doing jobbing carpentry. By one of those incredible coincidences she was best mate of another psychologist lass I had a brief fling with a few years earlier. She in turn was the ex-girlfriend of Speedy Akwawe, Georgie Fame's conga drummer from Flamingo club days.

It was cup final time in Islington and Arsenal were up against Leeds. We scrounged material from local rag trade factories and made giant bunting that we hung across Mildmay Road. Rob knocked up an Arsenal cannon and stuck it on top of his old J4 ex-police van. On cup final day he crammed eight of the lads into his van and set off for Wembley. They were soon stopped by a Police patrol car. The constable handed over his ticket. He'd been called back on duty and couldn't make the match. Rob bought another 3 tickets from the touts and got all eight kids into the final, which Arsenal won.

Back at the Action House it was coming to the end of the financial year and I was busy dealing with building inspectors and organising an Easter camp in Norfolk. We were basically struggling to survive and present ourselves to the council as a coherent organisation so as to obtain another grant. The wimmin rallied round with some local mums despite the fact that the single mums' playgroup idea had been superseded by the reality of a thriving anarchistic youth club for teenagers. We went along and attended the council meeting together with a bunch of the kids. Miraculously we won through, got a new, bigger grant and a much better building with grounds at No 6 Clephane Road, 300 yards from the creative dope den at Englefield Road off the Essex road in Islington.

We celebrated by going on a camping trip to Norfolk, putting up our tents on Bantock's nocturnal rabbit-hunting grounds.

There is a kind of chaos that ensues when inner city kids are released into the wild. There were a few days of total insanity. The kids didn't think much of our muesli and brown rice diet for a start. We had to send some of them down to the local shop for Kellogg's Corn Flakes and baked beans. We later found out they had been slipping packets of fags onto the shopping list. As it was close to Essex a few of my East Coast Scene chums turned up to give a hand and we ended up having a really good break from grimy old London Town.

The new premises at Clephane Road and the bigger grant meant we could expand our activities. A cluster of Essex drop-outs appeared and joined in. We were becoming a hip alternative to Social Studies courses, sitting about smoking dope and fantasising about the revolution. In our own small way we were at the forefront of change. There was an explosion of adventure playgrounds and progressive projects happening around London. Ours was special with its emphasis on creative activities as well as play. We had a motorcycle workshop downstairs, a music rehearsal room, a grannies' dinner club, an adventure playground and the comings and goings of more and more kids. One of them, an enterprising Artful Dodger called Clive would set up a cafe, in a cupboard in the corridor. Wandering mystics and truth-seekers were co-opted as willing volunteers an American lass, Lisa, who stayed around for a couple of years, Lutz a German guitarist. More and more Essex people turned up and lent a hand.

Johnny Goodes, a local lad who lived in the same street as the Krays' Mum moved in the upstairs flat with his girlfriend Paula. He was a manic mechanic with rust-crusted eyes who loved pulling old English motorbikes apart. Him and his mate Toothless Ronnie played atonal music on guitar and drums. They had genuinely filthy dreadlocks, very few teeth and were, I'm convinced, the first Punks in London. They hated anything pretentious, trendy or middle class. They were our working class local lads' conscience and we had to keep it real when they were around.

Martin Turner now had a proper playworker's job, Keith Holleyman became our treasurer and rented a flat around the corner. He also kept people supplied with mind-expanding substances, having once ridden a horse across Afghanistan. At one point there were 28 people crashing in his 3-room pad. Some friends of Martin had moved into Clissold Road, Stoke Newington, to a Student Community house. Soon our followers were squatting the rest of the street and it became the fairly well-known Clissold Road scene. The Action House had been running on a combination of my adrenalin and charisma which kept pulling more and more people in. I was running out of personal steam and with three powerful characters around I started to get sidelined, with Martin and Keith ganging up on me. It was an uncomfortable feeling and I expect my reactions exacerbated the situation.

Come the summer Martin took us on a tour of Scotland in an old GLC, BMC bus that we had bought. John Geddes insisted on lying under it every day with the engine running to get his quota of carbon monoxide. Plans were now being laid for Islington summer festival. Martin had the bright idea of a giant prick as a float with a stirrup pump spraying white emulsion. It was all starting to go wrong and I left. I was ready for another one of my downers.

I travelled about a bit, Maglet gave me a second heave-ho! and I moved into a tiny room on the Balls Pond Road and started doing some leatherwork to keep body and soul together. The Action House staggered on for a few months more but was eventually closed down by a small clique of Conservative councillors while the Labour comrades were on holiday – mostly as a result of Martin's stupid prick idea. We attempted to occupy the building. I used all my student activist tricks and got people involved, called up the press. It worked for a few days until a demolition crew moved in and took out all the floorboards.

A few days later Martin and I were giving some youth club girls a lift home from Clissold Road. As we drove past the entrance to Clissold fire engines were screaming towards us. The nucleus of the old street gang had set fire to what remained of their Action House. 150 foot flames leapt through the broken, floorless shell of the house – it was an entirely fitting send-off but sad all the same. The community that had been created continued, in its way, with many of the volunteers, workers and kids moving into Clissold Road, a street of legal squats that would eventually become one of London's longest lasting alternative villages.

I went back to the rut of my solitary existence, exhausted, disappointed by the hedonistic excesses of my co-workers. For me the Action House scene was something with genuine political significance. We were creating a community and building on the natural cohesion of teenage peer groups, who were our clients. Kids who had bunked off school for years were going back or learning useful skills in our workshops. Our web spread to progressive middle class newcomers, demolition men, Turkish restaurant owners, Jamaican mums, local shops and factories and the stoned-out intellectuals of the university scene and the good people in the local council who supported us to the end. It was all about preserving that nucleus of communal spirit that the kids gave us all before it would inevitably be broken up by love, work and their uncertain futures.

It's strange, but I can pass through that part of London and bump into old faces or pop into No 9 Clissold for a cup of tea with one of Clive's lads despite the thirty plus years of a dope-heavy and then class A drugs scene and umpteen bedhopping single parent scenarios. I heard another young lad say, "I can't think of anywhere else I would rather have been brought up."

A sad footnote. Johnny Goodes, now homeless and jobless, took a position as fitter/bodger at a local spot welding workshop. He got electrocuted and died in hospital the following day. A lot of people went to his funeral at a sad, soggy crematorium somewhere on the anonymous outskirts of London.

1972: PITT STREET SETTLEMENT, PECKHAM

Living miserably in the anticlimax of my tiny hovel off Balls
Pond Road, I got a phone call one day from a guy called Tony
Kirwen. He had been called in as a consultant when it was all
going wrong at Clissold. He had just been offered the job of warden
of the Pitt Street Settlement in Peckham, would I like the live-in job of
assistant warden? It was one of those February life changes that keep
happening to me. I went for a look.

The Settlements were just that. Upper/middle class do-gooder
charities set-up in areas of large-scale deprivation around the turn of
the twentieth century. The previous warden had been in his post for
nearly 30 years. He was the honorary fees officer at the Houses of
Parliament, taking the MPs' tea money. When the 4-5 square miles
south off Peckham High Street had been compulsorily purchased he
had pulled strings and his beloved Settlement was saved. It consisted
of a courtyard. To the right was a 17th century, dilapidated, impracticable but solid farm house opposite an early Victorian terrace with a
pleasing verandah onto the yard. At the end was a red fetton brick
rebuilt cowshed that provided a hall with four small rooms above. To
the left of the courtyard complex was a newly decorated Victorian
bay-fronted house that was to be my accommodation.

Tony was living above the office in the other house with his wife
Tottie. What gave the Settlement its unique character was that it was
approached by a series of chicanes of corrugated iron corridors
running through a vast building site in the very first stages of
construction that was to become the second phase of the notorious
North Peckham Estate where, 30 years later, poor Damilola Taylor
would lose his life. The bleak, red-bricked old London County
Council Sumner Estate backed onto the building site.

I started work the week *The Harder They Come The Harder They
Fall*" was showing at the Peckham Odeon. I didn't have time to see it.
It would be another dozen years before I got round to it. The youth
club consisted of a joint gang of black kids and skinheads led by
Danny Defoe whose sport was going around 'Paki bashing'. I found
them swinging from ropes in the old cow barn cum scout hut. I immediately bought a good quality sound system and stuck some of my
hippy rock and roll music on. The second night I danced and wove

amongst the tribe of young Tarzans as they aimed kicks at my head with their cherry red Doc Martins. Danny got closest to putting me out of action, leaving the polish from his boot on my forehead.

I set about organising the place. First, their own choice of music and light refreshments. Through my network, I found an illustrator who set up a screen printing workshop and knocked out our Pitt Street Gang logo on headed paper and T shirts. Johnny Roster, a great guitarist and friend of Martin Sheaton's came over and brought fellow musicians to do jam sessions, including one of the members of the briefly famous Curved Air. Danny turned out to be a competent drummer. Next we acquired an old scooter, made a silencer from an old oil can and clattered up and down the corrugated corridor. The local Bobbies turned a blind eye as long as we kept to our patch.

Major-General Someone was on our management committee and invited me for tea at his beautiful old pad in Harrow to give us some useful cast-off furniture and tools. He was a fit, funny seventy-odd and approved of everything we were doing. His wife was busy painting giant murals on the generous walls of the house. Far from being stuck-up members of the class system they were fun-loving souls who had obviously lived life to the full and would easily have fitted into a gathering of flower-power progressives.

For the first month I did nothing but work and I would end my days in a sense of hollow anticlimax. I didn't know a soul in South London and would occasionally commute back to North London on my motorbike. Maglet was back on the scene, now in her final year at Uni., but I wasn't seeing very much of her. She was always sweet and helpful with the mad project when she did come by.

The new community started to build. First I found an artist and his girl friend living in an old school house. A very happy smiling Rasta called Lenny O'Reilly used to come by and light up mega-spiffs and talk in a delightful but difficult Jamaican patois. One night when I was feeling particularly down after a hard day's slog entertaining the kids there was a knock at the door. It was Lenny with a parcel under his arm.

"Me got something for you, man". It was a pungent bundle of grass wrapped up in "The News of the World". I subsequently gave him some work demolishing the old tuck shop, which he did in two hours flat. Then there were other jobs. He was so quietly efficient, always watching my back, handing me my lost keys, that we became good mates and an effective working partnership. He moved into the downstairs back room and became the unofficial Assistant Warden's Assistant. He had a giant, valve operated sound system in his room and he became the "keeper of the dope".

His touching story was that as a ten year old he had been hanging out on the beach in Jamaica with the Rastas. One day, he had been done up in his Sunday best, taken by bus to the airport and without anyone telling him what was happening, stuck on a plane for England to go to live with his sister in Birmingham. To this day he still pronounces it as Berminam. He was and is, of all the people I have met, one of the gentlest of souls.

Next came Dave from Essex with his fresh degree and girl friend. Then I found black Lou, a middle class drop-out from New York who fascinated the kids with his lingo and ball play. Dave soon moved on after I took all the doors off the flat because I thought it was becoming too middle class. Lou moved in and Jackie Galliard joined him for a while, bringing her inimitable Wildean wit and a sense of domesticity with Dominique, her young son by Liam Laden.

My sex life started to become complicated. Jean, a pretty hippy from Essex days turned up to help occasionally and we became lovers. Then 18 year old Jackie Patterson, one of the ex youth club kids from Islington, took to coming over on weekday mornings to seduce me before I got out of bed. To top it all the dear Maglet was pregnant.

My Mum, despite her obvious desire to have grandchildren helped us through the abortion. I still wasn't ready to be a father. I wasn't stupid or wicked. I knew what it was to be a fatherless child and I'd studied Economics. I knew what the financial implications and responsibilities were. I was still living on the frontier of change, being paid by the government, but very much anti-establishment in my outlook.

I don't care what anyone says about abortions being easy on the man. I know it's the most traumatic thing that can happen to a woman but for the male there is no finality of grief, just a long and hollow existential sore that remains as a wound to the honour and the soul for a long, long time. To me children, like puppy dogs, are not just for Christmas, they are for life.

Pitt Street started to grow beyond its early definitions of a hang-out for a teenage gang. Younger kids started to come. I took the kids out for Sunday drives in our minibus despite not having a licence and off to Essex to watch live bands.

Once we went to Kent University with a couple of local long-hairs and some of the senior kids. Capt. Beefheart was playing with his very weird "Magic Band", most of them wearing cowboy hats. I was wearing my leather cowboy hat and had very long locks which had been plaited by Danny's sister.

We left the gig and headed up the M2 and stopped at the all-night service station. As we pulled out I saw Beefheart's tour bus had stopped over by the cafeteria, so I drove round in a big circle and flashed them up and turned up an auxiliary road by mistake at the head of which was sitting a Police Range Rover. I stopped neatly beside them and said in my best earnest voice "Where's the motorway, please?" The long-in-tooth driver nodded in the right direction.

"Thanks," says I, breathing a sight of relief and drove onto the motorway. Just as I hit the carriageway the Range Rover flew by and pulled us with blue beacons flashing. I rolled down the window thinking, "Bugger! How did they know I was a learner? They've let me get onto the motorway so they can throw the book at me." The kids were leaping up and down in the back shouting, "It's de Babylon'

"Shut up, you lot! .... Problem, constable?" Nice and polite.

"We've had a report that your people have been smoking pot in the service station." Must have been the cowboy hats.

"Beg your pardon, constable. We're a bona fide youth club. I can give you the phone number of the Reverend Clifford White, our chairman, if you like."

He looked at us closely and at the kids just as Beefheart's tour bus sped past out of the service station. Magically close shave for the bearded Captain.

Around this time, the Mangrove riots happened in Notting Hill Gate. It was centred on the restaurant but also involved a local GLC. youth club.

I got summoned to county hall by Dennis Maglyn to meet with his chief educational psychologist and someone else to discuss my ideas for running creative youth clubs as distinct from somewhere to hang out and play table tennis. He was the father of another old Essex face called 'Angel' Maglyn and I had visited the family's home in

Newcastle. I have a fond memory of me in my radical cockney cowboy outfit having a brush down in the red marbled gilt-tapped "members" toilets. Three months later a half million pound project, the London Truancy Centre Initiative was announced by the GLC, almost entirely modelled on the info. I gave them that afternoon.

On the way home I was sauntering down a back alley in the West End, looking for somewhere and slightly lost. I was wearing a cowboy hat and had a long roll of drawings crooked in my arm, looking from a distance as if I were carrying a rifle. At the far end of the lane, a Bobby appeared and we walked steadily towards each other in the middle of the road, like a high noon showdown. I was about to say, "Excuse me, constable," when he lunged at me with a grin and a fake six-shooter draw. It was my old school-mate Baz Wilkinson, pounding the beat from West End Central. He had been one of the brainiest, sportiest kids in school, but he was really happy sloping about the West End and kept getting threatened with the heave-ho for not nicking enough people. He had been on the other side at the 17th March '68 Vietnam demo.

Meanwhile, back at the Settlement we were becoming too popular – I would be woken up by a bunch of kids in my room bunking off school. The pressures of all-day contact with the kids was telling on me. I was smoking too much dope – Nepalese Temple Balls had just appeared on the scene. Too many hangers-on and hipsters were happening by my always-open door. Lenny was knocking out the music. I started to lose the plot, indulging in too grandiose schemes for our small flock, shooting off to too many meetings neglecting my contact with the kids, allowing someone to leave their dog with me while they went to America. which became a bait-object for the kids. Mistakenly I bought a clapped-out bus which got slowly junked in the street.

Jackie Galliard was still living with us and teamed up with one of my co-workers, Nick, who became the father of her second child. It was becoming a mini East Coast Scene and the place was too small. Tony was becoming more and more pissed off. He was a systems man, not a people person.

The crunch came one day when I was taking a bunch of smaller kids out in our old ambulance. Danny and his mates, who were being increasingly sidelined saw us and jumped in the sliding doors and ordered his two younger sisters out in a particularly nasty way. He was the older brother and his Dad was not in America, as he said, but actually in jail. I told him he couldn't do that sort of stuff around me and made him and his mates get out. I drove to my rendezvous realising that I'd really upset him. I stopped at a pub and rang Lenny, warning him to keep an eye on my flat.

"It's too late, the kids have come round and wrecked it."

It was time to pack bags again. I'd upset Danny's honour but he'd upset my pad. My relationship with the kids had failed and it was their message to me. I came back, handed over the keys and resigned there and then. I went back to North London and managed to find a single basement room unoccupied in Clissold Road, sharing a flat with a girl called Dawn, her tiny dog and a single mouse that wouldn't bother me as long as I left it some morsels out.

A week later Danny and his crew from the Pitt Street Settlement turned up with American Lou, larging it up but essentially asking me to go back. I turned them down. I'd given so completely of myself that I'd started to forget who I was. On top of that the revolutionary in me realised that I was stuck out there on the front line with a licence to amuse, getting more and more tied up in the bureaucracy of my job, being society's underpaid policeman while the researchers refined my ideas without acknowledgement and the creeping bourgeoisification of working class districts and the profiteering on property took place behind our backs.

I'd had enough of working for the government. I was about to become a full-time drop-out. It was to be twenty years before I earned enough to pay income tax.

1973: STOKE NEWINGTON

COLIN'S POST CARD

Clissold Cloisters, as I liked to call it, was a row of fifteen surviving houses from the 60s redevelopment mania. Opposite was a low-key old people's home, up the road a huge comprehensive school, further up on our side an old-style council public baths, sauna and swimming pool, at the top of the road, picturesque Stoke Newington Park, at the bottom a row of shops on Albion Parade and the Albion pub, run by dodgy Arthur and his handsome Barbie-doll girlfriend. The street was a mix of musicians, Essex and Action House drop-outs, a scattering of Scottish dope-heads and two fairly civilised shared houses under the auspices of Student Community Housing. Luckily Lenny joined me and found refuge in an abandoned room in No 5.

Martin Turner arrived fresh from nine months in the States while I had been slaving away in South London. He decided to build a wood-butcher's cabin in the back garden of No 11. The gardens actually funnelled into a no-man's-land where a huge metal ring was the site of a tethered barrage balloon in the First World War and where we used to hold wild parties with live music. I used to go out there early in the morning to practise Tai Chi. The incessant mechanical murmur of a waking city vied with the silence of a planet revolving timelessly in space.

We salvaged what was left of the adventure playground, blagged a multicoloured, semi-glazed door off a gentle giant of a demolition man and set to building a house on four telegraph pole stilts. Without a plan, our ideas started to clash so after the foundation stage I left him to it. Anyway I had to start earning cash. Somehow I got a job building a garage for a West Indian barber. Lenny and I were the oppos and a guy called Ray our driver with his corrugated tin Citroën van. Ray had special kudos because he had been living with a guru in India. Trouble is we had to wait for him to cook chapatis and smoke a ritual chillum before going to work. We were fucked before we started. Luckily the barber's missus noticed and she would knock us up glasses of hand-squeezed carrot juice and condensed milk that set us working like Trojans for the rest of the day.

Meanwhile Martin had completed his woodbutcher's cabin. A cross of telegraph poles 3 foot off the ground stretched between four upright telegraph poles. The floor was 9" x 4" timbers laid on their sides. A downstairs wood-carcassed room led onto a balcony with a hammock. The coloured glazed door was matched by small high-up perspex panels. Upstairs via a wooden ladder the bedroom was half sloping roof and half geodesic dome with more crafty windows and a clever use of some sheets of tortoiseshell plastic. Shaded by giant trees and with the use of facilities at No 9, it was the ideal hang-out for a Bohemian loafer and creative carpenter.

Later Martin would head off to film school in Bristol. His father had bought a series of houses in Scotland and another in Cornwall. When he returned to the UK he did not believe in profiting on houses – that is what they were, places to live, not property to buy and sell. As a result he had always sold a house for what he had bought it for. Martin took the same line and advertised his house in the *Sunday Times*: "Charming house, Stoke Newington, suit artist or eccentric, £200." He had to go into hiding from the number of phone calls. By one of those karmic twists of fate I would end up living there with my girl friend and future wife, who had ended up buying it.

Dear Maglet was still in my life. She was working with some light show outfit doing well negotiating the post-uni. trough. Pauline, John Goode's widow came by and we kept each other company on cold nights and I read her *Narziss and Goldmund*. Another ex-Essex lass, Shannon something-or-other, daughter of some liberal lawyer from up North, moved through the street shagging all the key figures in turn. She had been with the same lad throughout three mad years at Essex. Maybe it was her form of reality therapy.

Nearly everyone was dealing drugs. The music moved away from exciting West Coast rock or London multi-ethnic fusion to a sterile soul sound. A new conformity of fashion was creeping in. The hair got shorter, the colourful outfits turned to combinations of black, white and grey. Everyone was talking about being involved in video production, a bit like the computer obsession of today. Cocaine started to get used – but with my knowledge of the acid scene there was no way I was going to stick a suspect white powder up my nose!

Settling into an existence in London did not appeal to me at all. I had lived the first five years of my life under the pavement. I wanted out of a city that for me is either about earning or learning. I had done my two years plus of practical Sociology and I wasn't about to try and jump onto the bottom rung of a career ladder. I had applied for a community worker's job in Alexandra Palace and had got a phone call asking for a pre interview. It seemed like they really wanted me for the job. I was very tempted but knew it would be the beginning of a life stuck in London. My Mum had followed my Dad there aged 17, 40 years before and she was still stuck there despite all her efforts to escape. I turned it down and spent the next 20 years living honestly on the margins.

I was sitting in No 9 Clissold one day when this romantic looking French guy called François turned up. He was trying to find floor-boards for an old mill rebuilding project in Wales. This sounded more like my cup of tea and I took a ride back up to Wales. The mill was at the head of a tiny wooded valley outside of Corwen. Peter, charis-matic ex-owner of Compendium bookshop and builder had bought it with Linda, his missus. They had also bought a huge double fronted milliner's shop in town. Next to the mill was a double-decker London bus where a lass called Helen lived with her young lad and she took a fancy to me.

There was always plenty to do, cutting firewood, helping Peter, who was a building like a possessed octopus, digging the garden, entertaining the kids or just hiking about the hills. I would become a regular visitor over the next few years, mingling with a posse of creatives and ex- London dope dealers who were the advance guard of the British 'drop out and do your own thing' culture. A huge diaspora of young switched-on people headed for the hills and odd corners of the U.K. buying up deserted farms and funky buildings. Thirty years later the BBC would catch on and start making docu-mentary films about it.

I got a job with Peter's old oppo Winston in London. He was converting houses in Islington and ninety per cent of his workers were dope heads and Bohemians. He took me on as a carpenter. I had an innate skill with my hands but bugger all knowledge, thanks to Bert "The Shirker" Knight, our woodwork teacher at school. None of us, not even Winston, were pukka trained craftsmen but I always called it the Winston school of building where we all learnt our trade.

A postcard arrived one gloomy winter's day from Colin Dixon. It was from a country I had never heard of called The Yemen. He had been at Essex doing a conversion course from being a vet to being a sociologist. He spent most of his time shagging, driving his whacking great Triumph motorbike about or poaching. He had last been heard of heading for Cuba. His sister Liz had a flat in Ferntower Road, Stoke Newington that had become an early focus and crash pad in the Mildmay Action House days, until we swamped it out.

Colin's card simply said the Yemen is fantastic, medieval. Don't worry about money, just come. I got the map out and sussed a way of hitch-hiking via Sicily, Libya, Egypt, Sudan and the Red Sea. Wow! This idea really appealed to my sense of Boys' Own adventure and as an exercise in practical Geography. I hadn't travelled any further than Rome. I had also recently read T.E. Lawrence's *Seven Pillars of Wisdom*, so I was more than ready to escape the rut of dope smoking, coke snorting individualism that had descended like a somnambulistic cloud over the North London scene.

I started collecting jabs from the Hospital for Tropical Diseases and trudging round embassies in Kensington for visas. It was an entirely new, atmospheric experience, as if I were some intrepid explorer in the days of Empire stocking up for an expedition. There was a long, lingering after taste of the British Empire even then in mid-Seventies London.

Amsterdam

I've always found it difficult to leave London as if it were an island or country all of its own existing on a different temporal plane then the rest of Britain. This time was no exception. Weeks late, I went to say fond farewells to the Maglet. I couldn't take her with me; this was a man's mission, part adventure, part self-discovery. She bought me a big wood and brass handled Bowie knife for a leaving present and made me a beautiful card out of a picture of her and me. I'm still feeling bad and regretful even now 30 years later at the leaving and loss of her but a boy's gotta do what a boy's gotta do.

Getting on the bus to Liverpool Street station proved to be the hardest part. I left at seven o'clock on a dark London night. Keith Hollyman gave me some cocaine for the first time ever as a leaving "present". Some present! I couldn't stand still for more than five minutes. I was trying to get a 253 bus from Stoke Newington High Street, but I kept popping into the shop over the road to buy chocolate, sweets, fag papers etc. I missed three buses, the train to Harwich and the boat to Holland, ended up stranded for the night after a train breakdown – sleeping on the floor in a pub bedroom with a mercenary on his way to the Congo!

By some geographical quirk I was heading for Amsterdam, not that it was on the way to The Yemen but it was a good stepping 'stone' into another culture. I ended up staying on a houseboat with two American lads who had set off from Keith's Islington pad one year before in a VW camper en route to India. They had got stuck in friendly little ol' Amsterdam and were so stoned and ensconced they weren't going anywhere.

Another American, a girl called Becky was living in a civilised cream-painted German passion-wagon on the quayside. We teamed up and she would take me for terrifying rides across town in a tiny Daf car, mounting the pavement when the traffic got stuck. I was getting stuck too, with all the best quality hashish I was consuming. One evening in desperation I asked her to drive me out of town – more farewell mega-spliffs and I had such a dose of the munchies that I had to purchase a litre container of Vanilla Fla (a kind of cold custard) to stop me from eating the car. Picture Becky weaving in and out of the traffic, bumping up onto pavements, me with upended carton of Fla touching the roof.

Suddenly I was standing on a squeaky clean, fairly new round-about at the beginning of an autobahn heading towards Germany. The urban desperado seeking the last motorway.

1974: En route to Yemen

via USA Kaiserslautern and Malta vc

Where is The Yemen? Does anyone know? It's actually on the other side of the Red Sea from Ethiopia and bends round the bottom of the Arabian Peninsula and includes Aden, the old British coaling port. In those days it was divided into North: Democratic Republic and South: People's Democratic Republic; communist style. They had just had a nine year civil war between the supporters of the old Imam who could trace his line back to the Prophet and the socialists, supported by Nasser's Egyptian army and the Russians. The shaky Republic of North Yemen was just established. The country's one road ran through the spine of mountains that was bordered by the Ketama desert strip on one side and Saudi Arabia on the other.

It was going to be a mission getting there via three seas, 1,000 plus miles of Europe and another 1,000 plus in Libya, Egypt and the Yemen. I slept my first night next to a German autobahn in a park. In the morning I found an English expedition en route to Egypt. They didn't give me a lift.

I had the address of a guy living on a US Army base in Kaiserslauten so I headed there. I had cut my hair and straightened up my image in an effort to dig myself out of the dozy, dope-smoking trough I was sinking into. My version of looking straight was U.S. Vietnam lightweight army boots, blue dyed seaman's socks to the knee with jeans tucked in, a blue sub-mariner's anorak topped off with a Scottish army Tam with red bobble. I looked like an escapee from a Scottish tank regiment. I arrived at the barracks at night through a back gate and found a road barrier defended by a mix of black and white conscripts who were having a laugh riding up and down on the barrier pole – so much for security. They directed me to the American version of the NAAFI, a Jeep ride away.

A crap country and western band were playing to a handful of lumberjack lookalike white guys with very short hair outnumbered by super-big black guys all dressed in natty suits. Nobody took any notice of the weird Scottish trooper in their midst. I collared a bespectacled, intelligent-looking black guy who was bored with the show. He had heard of Corporal Blake so he took me back across the base past the circus of security troops to the military Police station –

Corporal Blake a mate of a hippy chick in London was actually a military copper!

I walked in the door. It was Saturday night so the place was full of pissed-up customers in handcuffs. In front was a raised counter about eight feet off the ground with a rock-faced, stony-eyed Sergeant with a hair style designed by an upside-down wind-tunnel. "Corporal Blake?" I said, trying to sound serious and as if we had something in common. Two slits of eyes moved to the left like machine-gun turrets and focussed on a uniformed mustachio'd bespectacled corporal in the corner. I sidled up and said, low key, like, "I'm a friend of Karen's, from London" He spoke without opening his mouth: "Cool, I've got a place you can stay, man. Wait outside."

Ten minutes later I was riding through an American military base in a massive military Police car. I felt like I was in a Paul Newman movie. Gerry was a working class Vietnam draft dodger. By enlisting he could choose his own unit – the military Police didn't get sent into battle. He was a vegetarian Buddhist who started the day with a bit of yoga and lived with a nice missus miles away from the base. Apart from sorting out drunks and car crashes they would get called out if the German cops caught anyone with dope. This meant the dope would get recycled straight back into the camp!

He took me to see some chums living on the edge of a forest. They were supposed to be on duty but they were stoned off their heads while the Grateful Dead was playing on their Jeep radio. No wonder Kissinger had to bomb the fuck out of the Vietnamese. The American army was useless – and full of a load of pacifist dope smokers as far as I could see. We were shopping at the PX, which was basically an American shopping mall. Gary stocked me up on some goodies for my travels including some Listerine, something we'd never heard of in the U.K., for a burgeoning toothache – courtesy of those long-legged ladies of Pimlico and their chocolate treats.

I meandered down to Sicily, looked for and didn't find Dante Maiorana and slept on some lumpy ground outside of town with a spacy freak I met there. I was on the foot of the boot of Italy like a ball about to be kicked into the unknown. To get across the Med. I had to book a passage to Malta with the option of going on to Libya, which was out of the way. What I really wanted to do was get a ship from Malta to Alexandria in Egypt. I'd started out my travelling adventures hitching a lift on a plane, why not a ship? At the dockside I met a nice older English lady with a VW camper waiting to board the ship. Her husband turned up, a gruff, sandy-haired Scot who was nevertheless kind enough to ask me to accompany them on board. Maybe he liked my Tam O'Shanter?

The couple lived in Malta. He was an ex-colonial teacher and had opened the first school in Zanzibar. He blasted most of my pie-in-the-sky social theories like grouse in the moors but still invited me to stay while I searched for a ship. Embarrassed by their hospitality I offered to dig out their basement and after a two-day shovelling exercise left a tidy, earth-banked room – pity about the stinky dead cat.

I spent days trying to find a ship, meeting loads of friendly Maltese, who had lived in places like Southampton but the same answer kept coming back, the Suez Canal was closed after the 1967 Arab Israeli war and there was no traffic. I did get as far as taking a dingy ride out to a giant Dutch ship with Sandy, and met the Captain, but not possible. I would have to book a ferry to Libya and leave behind the hot little outcrop of rocks with the friendly Maltese and their old, perfectly preserved Vauxhall Wyverns and Ford Consuls. I was heading for the unknown.

1974: LIBYA

Libya was a building site and I got out of Tripoli as soon as possible on to the desert road to Egypt. I got my first lift from two students who took me back to their Dad's farmhouse. They were dressed Western style in slacks and button down shirts. The Dad, Mum, sister dressed local in white voluminous robes. Me and the boys sat in a back room on a red-patterned carpet drinking Turkish coffee and smoking Benson and Hedges. It was the first day in Africa but I couldn't help thinking, "this is just like sitting in one of my mates' pads in Stoke Newington; all that's missing is the dope.

I blundered on and found myself in the desert for real with two smart Tunisians in a green Peugeot 304. They kept stopping every 50 miles or so and polishing the car to keep it cool. There was bugger all vegetation except for these big grapefruit lookalikes on spindly bushes that were inedible anyway.

I was dropped at the border and was in for a shock. Libya and Egypt had just had a mini-war and it said clearly on my passport Entry to Egypt forbidden via the port of Saloum. The port was actually a nasty concrete complex of ugly Russian-built border buildings in the middle of a lot of desert. The flooded, broken toilet block meant the area was surrounded by an ever increasing circle of turds in the bare desert. A single donkey stood docilely blinking with a five-legged hard-on. Phalanxes of Egyptian workers were passing in both directions all in white Peugeot 504 estate cars as if it were really an extension of the factory production line.

Coming in the Egyptians would be loaded down with crates of tomatoes, chickens, fruits, bundles of cloth and clothing – going out, air conditioners, fridges, TVs. The trouble was both governments were giving them a hard time and searching every car in and out. It was my first experience of the wailing, weaving din of the oriental bazaar. That's exactly what it was like. Impatient drivers, beseeching mothers, hard-face customs men on the take, armed to the teeth troops. As usual the innocent civilians were paying for the politicians' cock-ups.

Luckily for me all of the officials that had been banished to this turd-ringed circus of hell were more or less around my age, ex-radical students of the Nasser era and dying to practise their English on me and do their best to wangle me across the border. It would take three days to get the various permissions and my toothache was becoming painful. Customs officials, Police, immigration officers, bank clerks would see me and say, "Hey, English, drink some tea." Out of politeness, with nowhere to go and in the hope that they might help I would get through twenty cups of sweet, sticky Nanar mint tea a day, gasping with searing tooth pain as the three sugars to a glass chewed away at my exposed dental nerves.

My dormitory was the wood and glass-panelled, roofless bank booth stuck in the huge customs hall, looking a bit like it had been found on a classy skip in the City of London. My permission came through via some nice Egyptian intelligence officers and they ordered a passing group taxi to take me to Cairo. There must have been twelve of us crammed in the 504, shoulder to shoulder so tight it was more comfortable to sit sideways.

At a night-time paraffin-lit tea hut in the middle of nowhere an old, old man squatting in the corner with white skullcap spoke to me in broken English he had learnt with Monty's troops 30 years before. I felt strangely at home, remembering the Field Marshall's march-past at our old school and the rancid smell of hand-me-down, WWII army uniforms.

CAIRO

What a kaleidoscope of humanity, old and new, fast and slow, donkeys and cars, white robes and dark business suits; a capital of commerce in a supposedly socialist regime. I walked about for days trying unsuccessfully to measure it against my own view of a socialist utopia. The grand sweep of the Nile with its overloaded buses, bikes, cars streaming above riverside wooden boat builders working with ancient adzes on banana shaped biblical craft.

I stayed in the youth hostel with a clutch of Euro travellers, met a nice German girl who was working with a museum, went on outings in a red Mercedes with a fair-haired Egyptian who befriended us, into Old Cairo where kids threw stones at us, people from another planet. Matey boy turned funny trying it on with the German girl and we had to do a runner from his flat.

Hand pressed juice bars were a delight and *fool* - delicious baked, bean stew bought from roadside sellers and all the fabulous, fresh foods and salads of the Nile delta. Plus the domino-playing, hookah-sucking cafés where old men would ruminate around circular tables in the cool night air.

The trouble was my toothache was becoming unbearable. Kristina, the German girl, knew a nice trade union man who arranged for me to visit a dentist. There was a sullen queue and a young, big, brusque dentist. There was none of the "Oh, does it hurt, let me give you some more pain-killer." Out came the pliers and it felt as though I was being tortured to death by some demented Nazi. How I didn't black out I don't know. Five minutes later I was walking along the banks of the Nile clamping a very bloody swab between one less teeth. I went straight to a café, and smoked a hubble bubble, trying to imagine I was getting stoned.

It was time to make a move. I had left England with £90, which was starting to get thin. Andrew Jedwell mailed me a similar amount I had left with him and it gave me a homesick pang picking it up from the bank. I said farewell to kind Kristina and the mad mayhem of Cairo and boarded a train for the long ride south towards Sudan.

WADI HALFA – KHARTOUM

Hot wood
Train seat.
Black brown
Coffee cream
Big heart
Sudanese.
Chicken chatter
Camel men
Sedate city boys
With plastic sandals
An' saltpetre cigarette
Todd the Nod
Sleeps on
Midday sandswirl
Sucks the juice
From cracked
Mud brain
And blood bubbles
In my
Rubbery
Legs.

A plastic bag of tomatoes melted in front of my eyes with the twice-amplified heat of the desert through the train window. A donkey stopped dead on the banked levée of the Nile throwing its rider over its head and got a severe beating. Negro-featured Sudanese mixed with Egyptians. There was luggage and bundles everywhere. Stopped for a day at Luxor visiting timeless temples, trekking across fields up a sandy hot line of hills to avoid the tourist traffic to the Valley of the Kings, got bushwhacked by a trinket seller at the top of the pass. How did he know I was coming? – nearly threw his offered 'antique' off the cliff. Saw the majestic green flanked swathe of the blue ribbon Nile disappearing into a shimmering intensity of desert distance. Befriended a boy and had lunch in a lovely mud house with dovecotes and white winged birds on the roof.

More train south, slowly snaking through the sand, nodding off with the heat. Whitewashed identical stations with neat water towers for old steam trains in the middle of nowhere, christened with numbers rather than names. So British. Stops at bends in the Nile, assailed, thankfully, by hawkers and vendors of fresh foods and salads, big-hearted Sudanese shared lunches with me and at night slept crammed between baggage in the aisle.

Arrived after an age at Aswan Dam and Lake Nasser, a fantastic and highly necessary Russian-built project; trouble was that it had cut the road to Sudan. Now we would have to board a ferry for the trip across the lake. The engineless triple open-decked ferry had a tug strapped to its side for power and somehow it didn't go round in circles. The decks were stacked with merchandise. Afro hair-styled city boys on their way back from work in Libya had shiny new motor-cycles and ghetto blasters. A large troop of returning camel dealers with fine features, flowing robes and big knives were carrying pots and pans, baskets of chickens etc. etc.

There was basic catering of bean stew and bread once a day but as a traveller heading in the direction of Mecca everybody invited me to eat with them. My particular mates were a contingent of handsome tall negro Sudanese soldiers on their way back from exercises with the Egyptian army. We feasted on bread and giant tins of marmalade and Danish Feta with their Kalashnikovs stacked in the corner.

Stopping at night the quirack quirack of crickets mingled with a solitary guitar. An old Muslim man helped me cut my hot hair as we landed at the clean, tidy township of Wadi Halfa. Another long slow crowded snake of a train rumbled on through a monotony of desert – Reaching Atbara, halfway to Khartoum I hopped off ready to seek a ride across the desert to Port Sudan and on over the Red Sea to the Yemen.

ATBARA TO PORT SUDAN

SAND SLALOM

Atbara was a railway junction town, a bit like a cowboy town in a Western, battered, overloaded lorries, sandy adobe streets, open fronted tea houses and restaurants. And very hot ... I was instantly befriended by a young Police cadet in civvies who wanted to practice his English on me. He treated me to a fresh salad lunch and we went to the truck stop to find me a seat to Port Sudan. There was only one truck leaving and I had to scramble on board. Its load of lorry springs, tyres and general paraphernalia was topped by a couple of wild-haired Adendre dudes with strange bulbous-shaped swords in goatskin scabbards. I roasted the rest of the afternoon trying to find a comfortable spot for my bony bum. Somewhere I had acquired a pair of old leather-clad motorcycle cum pilot's goggles to protect my eyes from flying sand – long range desert patrol, here we go!!

We stopped briefly under a full moon star-spangled night. The Adendre shared yoghurt and bread with me and I gave them a US Army webbing strap to tie their swords together. I was dreading the next day, being toasted by a full day of sun. We stopped early in the morning by the slow coach railway plodding its knackered way West. In the shade of a hut a driver was sitting putting boiled milk powder in his tea. Being a bit of a mummy's boy National Health baby I had a sudden craving and asked for some. He obliged, spoke English and invited me to travel with him in the cabin of his truck, luxury no more roasting white boy!

At dawn and at night he would skin up a joint of marijuana using Benson and Hedges and Rizlas, but never during the heat of the day. Occasionally he would stop and deal some to a passing mate. This was home from home! Navigating in the desert is based on intuition, luck, following the tracks of others and hope. Myriad tracks plough through the sand following the line of the slow coach railway. We would follow, deepening ruts until the axle grounded, then we would skirt wide, making a fresh track in the virgin desert until we started to flounder. Stuck trucks would be towed out by others and this strange erratic constant caravan of individual trucks somehow navigated the 500 miles to Port Sudan.

Early on our driver broke his little finger and I felt such a wanker, what with all my revolutionary fervour and being unable to drive. I had travelled about the country in Billy Miller's Pickford's wagon when he was still doing long distance driving. It was the early days of the motorway network so we followed old 'A' roads up hill and down dale. Driving through the Sudanese desert I could suddenly see how new roads and routes had been opened up in days gone by.

Mohammed would pay for our snacks and meals on the way, always politely refusing my offer to pay. As well as stopping to sell some dope he would pick twigs from the toothbrush tree and show me how to us it by peeling back a half inch of bark chewing the end into a bristly fan and then scrubbing vigorously. The mild antiseptic properties of the sap provided the cleaning agent. Ingenious guy that Allah!

We arrived at the end of the sand desert and started to rise up a marginally green set of hills. A British regimental insignia was marked out by neat white rocks on an escarpment, matched by another, not so neat, in backwards-flowing Arabic script. It reminded me of the White Horse of squaddie Westbury, Wilts. Stopping at a rocky, spiky-bushed tea stop, a group of about four locals were on their knees on the stony ground praying to Allah and giving thanks. They milked one of their scrawny goats and gave me hot milk for my tea. I was awe-struck by their simple generosity and faith.

We arrived at a town and effectively the end of our desert trek. A proper working man's restaurant served meat, rice and fresh vegetables – onions. Mohammed asked me to lend him the money to pay.

"Don't be silly, I'll get this one." He wouldn't have it much as I insisted.

"You are a guest in my country. Would I pay if I were a guest in your country?"

"Probably, yes, you would," I thought. We left soon after.

"What about the payment?"

"I shall pay next time." I was en route to Mecca. I had to be protected and succoured, according to the law of the Koran.

We parted soon after in Port Sudan. I was so tempted to give him my knife, as he wouldn't accept any money, but I didn't and felt mean after his hospitality. The knife was an essential tool, weapon and source of hilarity, as I would later discover.

Port Sudan to Mecca

Port Sudan, a once-thriving Red Sea port was knackered and moribund because of the closure of the Suez Canal as a result of the Arab-Israeli war. A tidy town, nevertheless, inhabited by big, black beaming-faced Sudanese wearing loose foot-length pale cotton garments and beautifully crafted but simple slightly pointed slippers in snakeskin and various rich coloured leathers. Black crows lined the roofs where seagulls should have sat and in the market a woman drank blood from a pigeon's beak.

I found the one half-tidy hotel in town with a bar run by an old Greek lady called Mrs Tesseras. A garrulous half drunk doctor sat at the bar. She was soulful, sad, cynical but amused at this new type of traveller. She put me up in a small room at the top of her squeaky-staired building and I paid her with a handful of brass belt buckles I was carrying with my leather workers' kit. I would later immortalise this kind soul in my book *The Sword of Justice*.

There was a single ship going to the Yemen and I blagged a ride. It was Saudi-owned, Egyptian crewed ex-Denmark-to-Greenland ferry with central heating and no air conditioning. I watched while weak-kneed dockers loaded it with giant sacks of sesame and stacked refrigerators as though they were mismatched jigsaw puzzle pieces. We left port at night with a pronounced list and headed out into the humidity of the Red Sea, me catching fitful sleep on the sacks of sesame festering with tiny weevils.

The crew befriended me and I helped out in the kitchen in return for food. Abdul the cook taught me the rudiments of carrying out ablutions with the left hand and eating with the right. The snobby bursar got me to fix some woodwork. Later they offered me the job of ships carpenter. It was a romantic offer and I was very very tempted but we were nearly in sight of the Arabian coastline and I had to see my journey through.

We stopped in Medina, port for Mecca alongside brand new corrugated warehouses. Something told me not to bother getting off. I already knew that the modern Saudi culture was dominated by money and moral prostitution. It did not appeal to me one bit. A very bright intelligence officer came on board and questioned me and invited me ashore. I still declined, but later went for a saunter past huge stacked high warehouses with boxes of this and that. I managed to blag a tin of mummy's boy Dutch dried milk.

The next day we took on a thousand Yemeni deck passengers. The Egyptian crew would not give them cabin space because they were "dirty Yemenis". They had to make do with a single temporary toilet but I didn't see any dirt. I expect the accolade was left over from the civil war. Colin had told me of Yemeni mountain houses he would visit where the walls were lined with Egyptian soldiers' caps with bullet holes in them.

They were small wiry people with lovely faces and twinkling eyes. The men wore a combination of Yemeni Fulta – long skirt, European jackets and shirts and wound round turbans in a variety of colours. We docked by a single wonky crane. I bid farewell to my shipmates and I set foot on Arabia.

Amidst a milling throng of baggage totting Yemenis I was ostensibly at the end of my journey but I was actually at the beginning of a much longer one that would end up with me 20 years later living in an old Moorish village in Spain where the water masters of the Yemen built the Acequia water system that delivers water from the melting snows to every mountain field right were I am sitting hand writing these words.

1974: Yemen – Felix Arabia

The Romans called the Yemen the Garden of Arabia with its cool, sun-bleached mountains that attracted most of Arabia's rain. The remains of the Great Marib dam overlooking the empty quarter of Saudia was the fabled site of the Queen of Sheba's empire. In recent history the British had colonised Aden and not much else and the country subsequently divided into pro-Western North Yemen and pro-Eastern South Yemen. Most of the male population were now working in Saudi and Kuwait.

I crossed over the Ketama desert strip and headed through brown mountains with green valleys, pretty goat herd women showing their faces and small, squat, 3-storey, flat-roofed houses trimmed with bright colours all about. I soon got a ride from a German guy installing the country's first TV station. He knew Colin. It was easy to get a ride with one road in and one road out and a handful of foreigners under a tranche of aid agencies trying to institute development programmes after the devastating nine-year war.

I found Colin in Taiz, the Yemen's second city, living in a local hovel with paraffin lights and only a car-battery stereo, as was his wont – right in front of a rubbish pile. Despite inviting me out he was leaving for hospital treatment in Europe three days later with Dominique, the beautiful wife of a French doctor called Joel. He took me on lightning visits to meet Zahara Norman, who was sister at the hospital, formerly of Aden and Birmingham, with half her kids talking Yemeni and half Brummie, then the other volunteers, Tony Milroy, irrigation, Fernando, town planner in the capital, American Bob who was a nutritionist without a job so grew tons of best quality dope in his walled garden next to the State Security HQ. He took me for a quick hike in the hills to visit some tribespeople, gave me a lesson I never forgot on how to do a yoga headstand and then left me the keys to his house and a mission to placate the distraught Joel whose wife he had just nicked.

The house was very back-street and set in a square of identical other single and two-storey houses at the rear of some shops. The construction was relatively modern and full of 20th cantury rubbish, tin cans, wrappers, boxes etc.

Being a semi-retired community worker and ex-London bin-man,

I decided to do something for my new neighbours. I went up to the UN road-building depot, blagged my way in, got hold of a 50-gallon oil drum and was walking out with it on my shoulder when I got stopped by a Kalashnikov-toting guard. A big pow-wow ensued with some Swiss aid worker explaining I couldn't have the oil drum without triplicate permission from the capital, even though there was no use for it; my early into to the toothless tiger of the United Nations. And I thought the Swiss liked to keep it clean!

Yemen was a frontier of two civilisations. As with so many other unspoilt homogeneous societies on the geographical margins (Somalia, Afghanistan) it had been brought screaming into the 20th century via comrade Kalashnikov and the surrogate arms dealers of the CIA.

When I asked the British consul at a party one night why we hadn't colonised the rest of Yemen as well as Aden he replied, "My dear boy, if there had been anything here worth taking we would have taken it."

Yemen was considered the cradle of Arabic civilisation and has a written history going back beyond the Middle Ages. Its fertile mountain valleys supported a thriving and self-sufficient tribal culture. Oil had changed everything. Yemeni builders are master masons.

The country is festooned with tapering, three storey castle cum houses made from hand-hewn rock, complete with drainage pipes made from cut rock sections. That was why most of its men were working in Saudi or Kuwait, they were building modern Arabia. Bin Ladin's father was a Yemeni builder who ended up owning half the real estate in Saudi Arabia. As a contractor, he had built a very difficult road through the mountains. Old King Faisal was impressed and he got to build most of modern Saudi. Whenever he got to build a road he would establish a camp near a water supply and marry a local woman.

Once the roads were finished and hotels and infrastructure grew up, he owned all of it. Having become one of the richest self-made men in Saudi Arabia he died in a mysterious plane crash. His eldest son was then killed in a microlight accident in George Bush's Texas. I don't think Osama Bin Laden is much of a Buddhist but I think even he will get a sense of karma out of that one, or did he plan it? Those who were left were buzzing like bees up and down the one unfinished highway in trucks, pickups and motorbike taxis moving in this cacophony of honking horns and revving engines. Everyone was armed to the teeth, mostly with Kalashnikovs, but in 5 months I never saw or heard a shot fired in anger.

As well as the guns and bandoliers of bullets, every male carried a Jambia; it's a short, curved knife 2" wide at the hilt with a double convex handle of bone. Most are studded with well-worn British, golden sovereigns. They are carried in front in a sheath that protrudes from a wide belt or sash in such an obviously phallic position that it doesn't look rude. I made myself a sheath for the Bowie Knife from some local leather and carried in it a similar position. This delighted the Yemenis who would shout "Jambia! Jambia!" at me but would decline to touch Sheffield steel with hand-beaten magnesium/iron.

I went on gut-wrenching trips with Joel, puking out of the window with his insanely unnecessary French driving style, hobnobbed with other volunteers and went on mini walking safaris in the mountains.

There was this strange bush growing everywhere that looked like a privet hedge. It turned out to be Qat, a highly narcotic leaf that male Yemenis are addicted to. Every day around midday the qat market would open, signalling the end of the working day, for the males at least. Amidst great haggling, the slapping down of bunches of qat or cash, deals would be done. Men would then sit around in groups, usually indoors, weapons parked in the corner, selecting the youngest leaves and chewing them into a narcotic gobstopper that would get wedged in their cheeks. With increasingly bulging eyes from the speed-like effect they looked like a bunch of turbanned, lop-sided clowns.

Copious bottles of Coca Cola would be drunk and filter cigarettes chain smoked. A newcomer to the Yemen being met by a qat-chewing Yemeni on a mountain path with bulging cheek, popping eyes, carrying Kalashnikov and Jambia and gurgling out a green stained greeting would have good cause to be petrified!

Mike Hunter was an accountant for Whinney Murray – a quiet adventurer who would fly across the Yemen's half made roads in his yellow, armour-plated Mercedes, taking me on excursions to places like Hodeida and the sunken port of Mocha, home of the first Arabica coffee. His house in Saana, next to the Saudi ambassador's, was open door to the small band of volunteers and travellers in the Yemen, with his ex-RAF cook Mahmoud struggling to keep up with demand and chew his qat at the same time.

I met two American brothers, one a devout Christian, the other a dedicated dope head and long-hair called Joshua. One morning, after a particularly good night I awoke from a dream in which three Americans, a guy and two girls had appeared. In the dream I had got off with one of the girls. Joshua walked in.

"Hey, guys, I just met three Americans in the bazaar."

"Oh, yeah?" says I, sitting up in bed, "how many guys and how many girls?"

"One guy, two girls."

"Where are they staying?"

I raced into town, found them and invited them over. That night I slept on the roof under the stars with a lass called Laura; there's nothing like making a dream come true.

What is it about premonition and intuition? Was I living nearer to the Arabian night full of stars or was it that my head free of day to day toil and preoccupations was empty enough to enter onto the superhighway of the supernatural? What would we all do with our minds if we were not wasting time earning money or running around in circles bumping into each other? Turn more pages or commune with the sages?

I enjoyed the company of the cheerful switched-on Americans who had made it to that remote corner and took them shopping down to the Souk. The most original things on sale were obsolete muskets and rifles. I bargained the bazaar boys down so well we got three for the price of two. I've still got my old rifle, an Algerian/French Mannlicher from 1874 exactly 100 years old from when we bought it* It was genuinely fond farewells at the airport to little Laura, dwarfed by her long, well-used rifle.

Who needs mobile phones when you can do astral travel under the star spangled skies of Arabia!

* *A friend of Keith's, Roger, subsequently wrote a book about the history of the rifle and put down the date of first manufacture of the Mannlicher as 1876. I had to pull him up on that one!*

1974: Hitler Dead?

Joshua and I decided it was time to follow in the footsteps of Thissiger and traverse the Yemeni mountains for at least a view of the Rub-al-Kalil, the Empty Quarter of Saudi Arabia.

We set off from Ibb, the central town-cum-village, early one morning. The near-vertical path was knackering with our bulky rucksacks but cheerful women in multi-coloured gold and red brocade dresses raced past us with giant bundles on their heads. Apart from truck-driving, these handsome, unveiled ladies seemed to run the country. All the markets were operated by them, plus animal husbandry, field work as well as raising kids. They didn't seem to mind. They always had stacks of cash and basketfuls of fresh produce or plastic crap and bolts of cloth balanced on their heads on their way back to the villages.

We struggled on, two pale white giants gasping for breath, recognising plants similar to those in English fields, clover, thistle, grass. We arrived exhausted on a plateau of limestone clints and grikes. A small cluster of Yemeni fort houses stood nearby. We sat looking down on the Yemens single unpaved road a mile below, fantasising about shelling the cultural invaders of the aid agencies. A crowd of women and children soon gathered and was beginning to get agitated. We were probably the first white men they had seen up the mountain and they didn't know what to make of us. I had a nasty feeling they would soon start throwing stones, standard practice in the East when people don't know who you are, a bit like throwing stones at dogs to frighten them off.

Just at that moment an old guy came skipping by on the rocks and said "Wanna drink tea? Follow me." We got up, grateful for the interruption and followed him to one of the fort-like houses. He was wearing a white turban, a navy blue postman's jacket, a white fulta skirt and Chinese plastic sandals.

As we followed him I said to Josh, "Did he say that in English?"

"I'm not sure ..."

We sat with Abdul, our host, cross-legged on colourful mattresses with bolster elbow-rests in a room bare of adornment but with coloured glass in its tiny windows. Animals brayed in the ground floor barn below. Two daughters, one of them huffy, beautiful and sulky, served us tea. As we sat practising our pidgin Arabic he suddenly said, "Liverpool, fish and chips, Houston, Texas, good place, Saigon, also good place ..." Our jaws dropped. More words of English came out and he pulled out a British merchant navy seaman's book. Inside there was a photo of Abdul as a young man with Errol Flynn hairstyle, big lapelled suit and kipper tie.

He walked down mountain tracks to the south and had worked out of Aden as a stoker on British ships and travelled all over the world. His last trip was in 1944. He looked at us and asked, "Hitler Dead?" It was thirty years to the year since he had gone back to his village and had nothing to do with our civilisation since. He genuinely did not know the result of the so called 'World War'. Thirty years on again I'm wondering whether his grandchildren are still sharpening their Jambias and if his two daughters are growing gracefully old.

SPICE ROAD

Our journey took us across a fertile plateau planted with sorghum and maize, in the distance was a rolling fold of more mountains to bend our knees to. Two young women tended goats in a field, one in black, older, deeply beautiful, the younger dazzling, bright-eyed in a silver brocade dress. We asked directions. The younger lass was oozing at the sight of two tall, bare-armed, blond-locked white boys. Joshua's ears were burning beetroot red. "Hey, man, I think the chick wants to ball me!" Older, wiser Paul could see a group of armed Yemeni men in the fields half a mile away over the valley. I reminded Joshua about the bullet holes in the Egyptian caps!

We climbed on up and up through verdant water-cascading valleys, through welcoming villages that delayed us with glasses of tea from bright Chinese flasks and polite enquiries about where we were from. Joshua changed his nationality to Irish. Occasionally a pop-eyed tribesman with bulging cheek, Jambia and Kalashnikov would bound down the path towards us and grunt greetings through green lips, proffering a tasty sprig of qat.

The burnt, red toasted, friable surface of multi-million year old rocks folded and twisted in a purple distance. The narrow footpath merged into a smooth, polished, mildly undulating surface reflecting exposed geological layers, blue slate, purple porphyry, red metamor-phosed sandstone, greens, greys, brown. The polish was a puzzle. We were surrounded by disintegrating erosion. The path rolled on into the distance, two loaded camels wide and I realised we were standing on the Spice Road, polished by the footfall of animal and man for 2000 years. It was the only viable route around the hot deserts of the Arabian peninsula, skirting the margins in the high mountains from Ras al Khema in the far east of the Emirates, through Oman and the Hadramut and turning the corner at Aden, to Yemen and north towards the Levant and Jerusalem. This was the route of the Three Wise Men, but there were only two of us and we were still looking for knowledge!

KALASHNIKOV ENCOUNTER

YEMENI SHOOTING PARTY

An old Ottoman Empire Turkish fort suggested shelter at the end of a long day of trudging through marvellous mountains. We had to evolve a technique of creeping past villages to avoid time-consuming hospitality but as soon as we entered the fort it transpired it was occupied by a large family. A white-bearded and turbaned old man invited us in. Young children rolled dark eyes at the foreigners. A teenage girl served tea as we sat back gratefully on cushioned bolsters in the stout-walled fort. Through a small window more vistas of mountains marched across the horizon.

Incongruously a young man slouched in the corner in bell bottoms and loud pink shirt listening to Stevie Wonder on Radio Kuwait. We answered the usual "Where to? Where from?" questions and conversed in pidgin Arabic, Josh practising his long, laborious language lab. phrases while I spoke in the limited vocals of the qat-chewers. The old man was an out-and-out royalist supporter of the old Imam and suddenly said the Israelis were "Ta mam" – good. That's unusual.

"Why?" we asked. Because they had defeated the Egyptians who had spent nine years trying to subdue the royalists. He asked me to make a copy of the crude map I was drawing "in case there was another war."

We stayed overnight and early next morning we assaulted the steep, as Mohammed would say. (Allah bless his name!) Young girls were already on their way downhill, eyes twinkling under giant loads of fresh thistles gathered while we snoozed. Arriving gasping and grateful at a tiny cluster of stone houses growing out of the rockscape, shaded by a single tree we sat, back to the wall on a flat threshing floor. The scene was Biblical. An old man exhorted a white ox that pulled a huge stone around in circles while a clutch of kids tossed grain in the air with wooden forks, the wind winnowing the chaff.

The idyll was broken by an unusually red and bare-haired Yemeni male who kept appearing and reappearing, agitatedly jabbering at us. I was so pissed off with the interruption that I shook my fist at him and said "Me and you punch up!" Minutes later he re-appeared with a rough, wool army tunic on, pointing a Kalashnikov at us and shouting "Yella, yella." – get out of the way – to the villagers. Joshua's ears turned deep beetroot red.

"Don't move, don't say anything," I murmured. We were literally sitting ducks. But, just in time, Lady Luck presented a handsome-faced fellow with a natty turban carrying a Chinese flask and two glasses. He squatted in front of us and poured us a cuppa. Life's full of surprises!

Polite chatter rolled around the usual "Where from? Where to?" theme. He didn't think it was wise us going any further towards the fabled desert of the Empty quarter because we were close to the border with the communist South and there were bandits about. His questions started to get political.

"The North Yemen – good?"

"Yes, lovely."

"South Yemen good?" A diplomatic, "Don't know, haven't been there." He returned to the theme of our travels. It really wasn't possible to go on towards the frontier town of Riad. Joshua suddenly said in that big, unintentional but bullying America way, "Well, we're fucking well going there."

Our handsome host shook his head. "La!" (' no!') and produced a time-polished Webley 45 revolver from the folds of his skirt and pointed it at Joshua's face. His ears nearly exploded with the rush of beetroot red colour. I hastily concurred with our host and we were invited to his house. He was effusive in his hospitality. More tea, biscuits, photos of him riding on a tank during the revolution, a trunk full of belts of large calibre machine gun bullets, a small arsenal of weapons including an interesting looking long barrelled Czech rifle, no doubt for hat-holing practice. I politely discussed the weaponry with my cadet force knowledge of shoulder thumping Lee Enfield .303 live target practice on Kent marshes.

It turned out he was a milita man, one of many guarding the small paths and passes to the south. I asked for some leather and two grizzled old men produced some thick cow hide. I pulled out my hippy leather worker's tools and knocked up a passable imitation of an English army officer's holster for the Webley 45 – I wonder if it was a relic of the bloody British withdrawal from Aden.

Mustapha was much pleased and invited us for a walk around. We set off with comrade Kalashnikov, Mustapha carrying the Czech rifle followed by a gaggle of small kids.

Joshua said, "Hey, man, they're taking us up the mountain to shoot us!"

"Don't think so, with a classful of kids in tow ." Matey Mustapha settled himself in a smooth hollow of a rock and sighted a clump of brown cigar-shaped bull rushes a hundred metres below. A burst of seeds exploded with his crack shot. Josh and I looked sideways at each other. Mustapha offered me a go – nice try, Paul, but the target remained standing, a lone clump in the shadow of the multi-million year old mountains.

A month or so later riding north in a pickup full of seriously armed militia their leader demonstrated Yemeni sharp-shooting. He took an oil can, removed the top, split a twig, set the top in the cleft and rested it back inside the can, which he placed twenty feet away on the other side of the road, which was not completely empty of traffic. He squatted down, pulled the trigger, missed. He tried again and missed. He swapped weapons with one of his lads and drilled a neat hole straight through the target. I stopped wearing hats after that.

The next day Mustapha escorted us to a small weekly market under unusually green mountains. A fine-faced young sheikh with a Parker pen in pale blue suit jacket over white robes scribbled elegant letters for a queue of locals. A clutter of clobber ranging from cheap Chinese plastic to sticky-sweet Iraqi dates was on sale. A demented-looking character in a heavy great coat hovered in the background dragging a ball and chain, the local 'magnoon', village idiot or petty thief. He would have been on a sort of Medieval community service – but there were no dancing bears.

We congregated with the Sheikh, Mustapha and a room full of armed militiamen. They were holding their weekly social and lots of Kalashnikovs. The assortment of weapons included a British Tommy Gun. We were treated to tea, dates and dry Chinese biscuits while ball-and-chain man sat in the corner getting passed leftovers of qat, food and tea. I wound up our hosts by asking which of their lovely weapons could shoot furthest most accurately, remembering stories of Lee Enfields sniping at one mile. They all got up and went outside. We were left alone in the room for so long that we got up to leave. An angry sentry ushered us back in. The sound of shooting came through the window. We looked out. Two women were grazing a goat on a flat meadow. Between us and them a group of militia were aiming their weapons over their heads at a spot high up on the mountainside, testing the range and accuracy of their weapons!

On another hike I had found a tiny mountaintop mosque-cum-guard post. Inside the diminutive holy dome a dried-up bottle of Stephens' Ink was co-occupant with an empty dove's nest. That was a homesick pang because the Stephens' Ink factory next to the Arsenal football ground was 500 yards from my Mum's house in Blackstock Road, London N5. Outside of the window was a pile of rusty food cans all with bullet holes in them! – Yemeni tin opening seemed to be the national sport.

BREAD AND BREASTS.

Parting from our militia chums we meandered across the non map of Yemeni mountains back toward the one half finished road.

We found a confluent of valleys and a flat green meadow to park ourselves for a last night under the stars. I scaled a solitary spiky acacia tree for a dead branch to make a fire and we ate the last of our food supplies with hand baked sooty chapatis. As I lay back under a sky full of more stars than I had ever seen chilling in the thin but groovy Yemeni blanket I had traded in for my bourgeois sleeping bag Joshua said, 'Wow man you see that star'

'Where'?

'Over there next to the other one'!

Good job we didn't have any dope to smoke or I would have been looking for it too!

Next morning I went for water to the nearby river. A trio of girls in red tribal dresses squealed, dropped their pots and scuttled off screeching. Back at the last embers of fire we had just made a cuppa to go with our not breakfast when we noticed a figure detach itself from a busy morning path a mile up the mountainside. An old man approached in tidy but well weathered skirt shawl and turban.

"Salaam Aliakum," (peace be on you) he said reaching inside the folds of his clothing and presented us with a large nan bread for our breakfast turned and hiked up the mountain. It was probably his day's food. Another example of humiliating hospitality from noble people with next to nothing. In Islam honour is everything. No wonder the Americans are having a hard time in Iraq.

We trudged on over what we reckoned would be our last mountain. All those useless afternoons of map reading at school cadets were paying off.

Rounding a bend of giant lumpy boulders we were suddenly confronted by a gaggle of unveiled women. Their leader was very charismatic and agelessly beautiful. She immediately took hold of a pinch of Joshua's arm and was very amused. She led us round the bend with her gang of about five other women all dressed in black which usually signifies marriage. We entered a sooty house built

154

between two boulders. An old man in a blue Turban scowled from an upstairs window.

They sat us down at the end of the room and fired questions at us while their ringleader pulled out her handsome breasts and started feeding a baby that appeared from nowhere right in front of my face whilst staring straight into my eyes. I was doing my best to look the other way in the confined space while Joshua's ears were going beetroot red again. Suddenly all the women started pointing at him and then at the youngest lass in the room and up towards the ceiling.

"They want me to ball the chick!" he said.

I looked up and saw a tea tin on the shelf above his head. "They want you to pass her the tea you jerk".

Two younger women entered in blue robes with heavily kohled eyes, they were both mountain flowers. They had the usual gummed up eyes that all young Yemenis had and we always carried ointment for. Joshua administered it with quivering hand. Meanwhile ageless beauty woman was still enthusiastically feeding the baby in my face and getting more excited. I couldn't help myself and started to say the kind of things that I would never say to a woman who spoke the same language. At this moment of extreme and oblivious passion the old man walked in and said, 'Masalaama.' (Goodbye!)

We hiked down the mountain in a daze admiring the endless vista of green brown purple peaks and hit the Yemen's only half road right by the German road building camp where we were treated to a slap up meal in the canteen and a luxury lift back to Taiz – orbital transfer time!

What a lucky and lovely time I had in that medieval society. I never felt a moment of danger, had my bag returned to me in a street restaurant a week after leaving it there, helped myself to a tin of dope in Portuguese Fernando's house, the city planner for Saana and couldn't find him in his 10' x 10' garden of giant dope plants next to State Security HQ, met some super switched-on people some of whom I would know for the rest of my life and met a lusty-voiced, red-haired, slender-waisted lass from Paris for some spontaneously vibrant sex!

Sometimes lonesome in Taiz I would visit the flat of Sister Zahara Norman and her half Yemeni, half Brummie daughters above her husband's closed dental mechanic's shop.

They had escaped from communist South Yemen by donkey

through the passes, emigrated to England, lived in Birmingham, him a dental mechanic, her a nurse, had half their family and then returned to the Yemen after the civil war had the second half of their family and set up a dental repair business. Of the six daughters, three spoke Brummie and three Yemeni. He had retired to a small hut in the country, living with his mate and an old rifle growing fields of veg. and receiving his family on occasional Sundays. There were two older brothers who were away "training in Lebanon". I helped about the flat mending broken sinks and gadgets, feeling at home with the chirpy lasses from Brum. One day one of them said "Eeh, don't e just look like Roy Woods from 'Wizard'!" So much for my straightened image!

I got on best and respectfully with 14-year-old Yemeni-speaking Fatima – on a mutual wavelength level. A year later Zahara turned up at my Mum's one and a half up, one and a half down in London with Fatima. I tracked them down to another older sisters' flat in Hounslow. I was a street gypsy at the time, hustling around with my new/old ex GPO truck and too stoned to be sensible – and made an idiot of myself. Later it struck me that there was only one reason that she had taken her daughter to my Mum's – first love and thoughts of marriage. The image and thoughts of the pure love of Fatima has haunted me with "what ifs" ever since but at the time I was still searching for normality, or was it just learning to live on the crossroads of change.

30 years later whilst finishing my novel "The Sword of Justice", partly set in the Yemen and running my mobile library/tea shop at a muddy beach festival a sympatico guy turned up and started building intricate irrigation ditches. Later over a cuppa and chatting about Yemen it turned out that we knew each other. It was Tony Milroy, irrigation adviser from Taiz. "Paul Goodchild, the guy who turned up and ate all my food!" Thanks for feeding the pirate/pilgrim, Tony.

He told me the devastatingly tragic news that two of Zahara's daughters had been burned alive in their own homes – probably by their fundamentalist brothers. She was living somewhere in London. Tony never got me the address and I didn't find out if Fatima was one of them, but I dedicated my pro-Islamic novel The Sword of Justice to Zahara and her two daughters.

ETHIOPIA

Leaving Yemen was hard. I applied for so many exit visas that the immigration Police chief threatened to have me arrested the fourth time round. I wended my way south with Geoff, the last of the three Americans. Mocha was the old trading port of the Yemen from whence coffee reached the West. It had sunk into the sea fifty years before and had a handful of surviving green-painted houses with graceful cracked wood balconies. The rest of the place was a humid, soupy-sea'd dump of tin huts, workshops and shops with giant fridges stuffed full of illegal lager, mostly "Harp", the beer no-one in England would drink. A solitary pier received nothing deeper than a motor launch or an old wooden dhow. Geoff had to swim out to a freighter half a mile offshore and towed a crate of beer back on a polystyrene float with a rope clutched between his teeth. Good teeth. Great swimmer!

We booked passages with a couple of German kiddies on the dodgiest boat on the Red Sea. We paid in dollars, not many and met on the pier in the dark. The high prowed sailless sailing dhow had a thumping great long-stroked diesel engine and the hold was stacked with old school rifles – we were not only sailing through the night in a busy shipping lane with no lights or navigation but gun running as well. Good job the Suez canal was closed otherwise it would have been a cross between Russian roulette and crossing a motorway blindfold.

As it was, flapping through the steamy soup of the Red Sea was relatively straightforward to start with apart from trying to find a comfortable seat on a cargo of scrap carbines. The 1000 year-old design of the dhow ploughed its own course under a sky full of stars as we Euro travellers nattered through the night. I dozed off and woke to an eerie silence and a sense of rocking to and fro. The muggy atmosphere reminded me that I wasn't dreaming but in a peacetime nightmare! The engine had broken down.

With poor swimming skills, a white skin in a desert latitude sea with strong currents I started praying and apologising to my dear Mum for being lost in a boat like my brothers. Then, as if the light was being switched on by a beneficent dreambreaker, the engine started and I dozed off to its slow-motion beat and awoke at dawn after what seemed like minutes later and witnessed the low, rocky shoreline of Ethiopia. We glided effortlessly into the organised French military harbour of Djibouti, perched on the point of the Horn of Africa and tied up alongside a French destroyer with our cargo load of rifles exposed for all to see.

We scrambled over the grey destroyer decks expecting an attack from someone but everything was completely quiet. We registered our presence with an out-of-place gendarme in pill-box Képi and khaki uniform in a tiny concrete hut. He didn't seem to care less and we left to sit and drink tea and eat fruits in a stylish colonial town centre with a bunch of pro-liberation locals.

ETHIOPIA - KENYA

THE HOUSE OF HAILE SELASSIE

The American lasses had told me about an old English lady, Mrs Keneally, who ran an unofficial hostel on the lower flanks of Mount Kenya. I had intended to go north to Lebanon and probably trouble so that's where I was now heading with my Bartholemew's map, the map with occasional, blank, white gaps where no British army surveyors could (or would) go, usually due to stroppy locals – Afghanistan and Somalia for example.

I travelled by a variety of means, train, slow truck, busted bus through a landscape first rocky dry then tropical verdant. I saw horsemen with high medieval saddles, their beasts with long, banana-shaped uncut hooves like uncomfortable clowns' shoes, thin prostitutes in the remotest Ethiopian truck stops. Eating meagre pancakes of fermented maize and transparent lentil gruel. It was the most botanically verdant country I had visited but the hungriest.

At a rainy truckstop I gave my T-shirt to a shivering mother with child. In the dusty town of Harar young lads went around with bushy afro hairstyles. I couldn't work out whether it was the local traditional wild man haircut or whether it was a belated attempt at aping 1970 American styles.

The revolution had just reached Ethiopia and Col. Mengitsu had arrested Haile Selassie, Lion of Judah, King of Kings etc. etc. It was to be the end of a 2,000 year old dynasty. He was reportedly locked up in his palace in Harar so I went round for a visit. There was a fairly nondescript two storey house in a sort of French provincial style, a couple of soldiers and more young dudes in monster afros – no sight of his Highness. It was a bit like going to Buckingham Palace and expecting to see the Queen!

If the guy couldn't sort out a decent blacksmith for his horses or feed his people from Nature's bounty, then it was time to go, crown or no. In the smallest of towns with no other signs of Western civilisation I found Italian coffee machines, a lasting legacy of Mussolini's 'new' empire. At mud hut corner cafes embarrassed ladies made cups of blacker than coal coffee. Luckily for the Italian coffee fanatics, come centuries ago Yemen's coffee masters had discovered qat, which the

Ethiopians were good at growing; and had become so good at growing that the entire male population were addicted. Goodbye coffee, goodbye Mocha. Meanwhile the Ethiopians had taken to coffee so a simple agricultural swap had taken place.

Leaving Ethiopia was also difficult, for different reasons. Some bright spark, no doubt some dim, just-out-university do-gooder working for an aid agency had dug up what pathetic road there was and installed concrete drainage pipes every couple of hundred yards. Trouble was the laid-back road builders had followed their instructions to the letter and the road, the site of the pan-African highway, was unusable. I had to cover the last 20 km on foot, scanning the deserted semi-desert of stunted spiky acacia trees for potential attackers.

I only managed to meet a couple of wandering women in long robes and head-dresses, but there didn't seem to be anywhere to wander to. I arrived at a low rise covered in slightly bigger trees and stopped for a breather, looked down and a scorpion was at my feet. I stamped on it super-quick and then thought, "Why did I do that?" There was only me and the scorpion in about a million square acres.

A rumble of truck engine sounded and like a mirage a neat green truck with shiny wheels appeared. The Somali driver took me on board for the next two miles. There was nothing to mark the border but a giant, colourful "Guiness Is Good For You" sign. Welcome to Kenya.

MRS KENEALLY - MOUNT KENYA

After taking tea with the daughter of the mud hut village policeman I headed south towards Mount Kenya in a variety of transport, pickups, trucks, bursting minibuses. One long ride was through another million square acres of acacia trees struggling out of the sandy soil. Here and there a handful of scrawny, skeletal cattle grazed guarded by big-eyed boys in rags. We pulled in at a two-mud-hut truck stop. I'd always been a bit of a vegetarian by choice, meat-eater by necessity. In this little wayside fundook with its insufficient thatch and smoky walls there was only one thing on the menu: cow! There wasn't a vegetable within 100 miles in any direction. I was there that I realised what a bourgeois, land-of-plenty concept vegetarianism was.

My last long ride was on the back of a crowded pickup with amongst others a giant friendly Ethiopian who we called "The Champ". He was on his way all across Africa to the Congo to watch the 'Rumble in the Jungle' between Mohammed Ali and George Foreman. I stopped off at the village of Naro Maru and plodded up a long dirt road towards the flat snow-topped splendour of Mount Kenya.

Mrs Keneally's place was a single storey clinker built timber house with a deep veranda facing onto a passable lawn surrounded by flowers and odd African bushes. I found Mrs Keneally a grey haired, fair-faced lady in her seventies in a kitchen annexe with a very black-faced Kenyan wearing a red fez.

"Make him some porridge, Wangi," she said, before I could open my hungry mouth. I'd never had porridge made from flour but it tasted great, swamped in milk from Mrs Keneally's cow.

She had come to Kenya in the 1920s as the wife of a vicar but as soon as the arrived she fell in love with Capt. Keneally, playing tennis with one leg and one arm at the Nanuki Club and left her husband forthwith. Captain Keneally had got himself machine-gunned in the last week of the First World War in German East Africa (later to become Tanzania). They built up their own farm, had three daughters and he had died about three years before. The daughters sold the farm from under their Mum and tried to move her back to England to enlist in an old people's home.

She refused to go and given that local Africans didn't like living in European houses, she squatted her own farmhouse and kept on about half a dozen horses which were her great love. She made a living providing self-catering accommodation or camping to passing travellers. We got on really well and I settled into life as her handyman and camp co-ordinator – basically hob-nobbing with the clientèle. There was a steady flow as travellers passed her details to each other on the road. There were a fair number of Americans and as the Swiss Army Knife had just appeared as an essential appendage of the true traveller, I made a living making leather pouches for the passers-by.

Mount Kenya itself was a bit like Trafalgar Square – a must visit kind of place so I stayed well away and busied myself being one of the lads about the bush with the Africans. One of my 'chores' was to ride Pawpaw, an ancient cavalry horse, to pasture, usually with some RAF personnel in some old ex-colonial farmsteads. I would ride the plodding Pawpaw over with a couple of other horses through a green highland landscape twinkling with the new corrugated roofs of mud-walled houses surrounded by a cluster of cows overgrazing the once-lush pastures of European farmers. We would spend pleasant after-noons while the horses cropped well-watered lawns and then plod back.

Not much of a rider, I would try and get Pawpaw to perform but he was totally impervious until the last mile when he got a waft of his waiting oats. I'd rise in the saddle and thunder along in a full-pelt cavalry charge with the old trooper.

I decided to visit the capital, Nairobi, not least to start organising the journey home. It was only £80 to fly so I decided to borrow the money from my old Essex and Stoke Newington squatting pal Martin Turner. The super-slow train from Naru Maru took two days to do the 180 miles to Nairobi so I hitch hiked. I got a lift in a Bedford bread truck painted in blue and white check just like the white sliced steam loaves it carried. Elliot's crap white man bread was still big in post-colonial Kenya. Nairobi's ring roads reminded me of outer London, neat dual carriageways, roundabouts with flowerbeds criss-crossed by barbed wire, to stop the Africans walking through them. The European style houses were occupied by Indian families, pretty much like the outer London ring near Heathrow.

The city itself was a neat enough collection of post war colonial buildings surrounded by shanty towns and with sprawling, open-fronted Indian shops selling everything, grains, clothes, tools, tins, ropes, gadgets. Tinny Kenyan Hi-life beat out from rickety wooden tea shops. Back street offices offered a variety of travel deals all over Africa and the world. City Park, a fair imitation of a British city park was a crossroads for travellers. All kinds of trucks were parked up in the car park – VW campers, snout-nosed sand-yellow German army trucks, zebra striped Mercedes and Land Rovers. A campsite supplied more traveller revellers to mingle with and tell tales of their travels and smoke the dirt cheap Kenyan ganga.

I couldn't help but think that the well-organised couples in their funky motor homes were actually like alternative suburbanites – I had even dispensed with my sleeping bag months before and, a bit conceitedly, saw myself as one of the foot soldiers of the frontiers of travel. I had, after all nearly had to swim the Red Sea and walked in from Ethiopia!

A second congregation point for all the travellers was an open-sided, wonky-tabled Kenyan cafe poised on a piece of waste ground near some of the tidy Indian houses not far from the Park. Roastie Toasties served three things: tea, bread and eggs. The bread became toast on a huge wood-fired hot plate. Eggs came poached, boiled, fried, omelette, scrambled and with a touch of cuisine Francaise, French toast.

I was having breakfast one morning when a chubby-faced, short-haired, sweatshirt-wearing geezer in shorts started chatting to me. He was a cheerful Londoner called Dave Perryman who looked more like an off-duty copper than a traveller – actually, he was on his bike. He'd been all over Europe from Greece to Sweden and worked there, flew Copenhagen, Gatwick, Heathrow, Nairobi without a stopover as he had nothing to say to England apart from stocking up on Rizlas. Trying to board a Greenline bus for Heathrow with his bike the driver said "You can't bring that on here, mate."

Dave dismantled his machine, popped all the heavy bits in his specially designed anorak, borrowed plastic sheeting from some builders, wrapped up the frame and wheels and got on the next bus. I was the first person he'd met in Africa and we would end up as pen friends for the next 30 years. I rode back north, first with a couple of Indian businessmen in an old Merc who were discussing house prices in Birmingham. They should have been worried, because Idi Amin was busy kicking out all the Indians from Uganda. We passed Dave on his old school drop bar touring bike.

Later, I was stood on a hillside junction and he came by again "Sorry, can't stop, see you at Mrs K's."

We yo-yo'd north and he turned up pink-faced later that night. John and Alison from Birmingham showed up later in their Land Rover and we had a month of hanging out together in a small oval cottage in Mrs Keneally's grounds. John would put the Land Rover's sound system through the window and a white pony would join in with its head stuck through the window too.

I got recruited by another oldish English lady, married to a high court judge, who was opening the Mount Kenya Youth Hostel. She needed a sympathetic builder. She had an American girl from Tucson, Arizona running it in another old English farmhouse further up the track. The roof needed fixing but the big problem was that the generator kept getting stolen. Dave was winner of the Silver Trowel on the bricklaying course at Watford Tech. and a pukka bricklayer. We found some rocks, about four courses of bricks, bought some timber and 6"nails and set to work. This was going to be easy after building Action Houses for inner city vandals in London. We were short of sand so we started excavating in the river. Dave suddenly looked up and said, "Fuck me, Paul, I can't imagine doing this on a Wimpey's site, can you?" I nearly drowned laughing.

As I mostly didn't have a lass to snuggle up to I would get up early and have a shower powered by the fire-under-the-oil-drum system. One day I opted for a cold douche in the river flowing from Mount Kenya's snowy peaks. The expression 'to freeze your bollocks off' is an accurate description because that's exactly what happened – they don't like being cold so they retreat! I can just imagine some twisted transvestite walking around with a bag full of ice strapped to their bollocks.

Around this time we heard that Mrs Thompson had an "accident". We visited her in hospital with a very messed-up face and she was coy about the causes. We realised later that President Moi and his bunch of crooks were busy consolidating their power – attacks on the judiciary were par for the course and Mrs Thompson had probably got herself duffed up by some of his thugs.

We treated ourselves to a night out at the pictures – Young Winston was showing. That guy got everywhere and there were a lot of survivors of the Empire who turned up.

Dave left for the coast and the Muslim island of Lamu. I was going to join him but got sick and sat in bed reading Dr so-and-so's book on apple cider vinegar cures in Vermont. Pity about the lack of apples in Kenya.

One morning I woke up to find that Dave's beloved bike had disappeared! I felt so guilty I went to the Police station, reported it and scoured the local townships looking for it but that was the last we ever saw of it. Dave subsequently travelled on through Africa, ending up in Rhodesia as a train driver and managed to get himself busted on Christmas day.

He took a ship from Mombassa to Bombay, toured India and followed his parents to Australia. Working class anarchist vegetarians, they had ridden bikes to India and then settled in Australia. Dave still lives in their old house in the national park south of Sydney and works part-time as a cabbie. He once said "I'm too busy to go to work, Paul." He's recently graduated as the only male member of a Women's Studies course! He is also a fanatic beer brewer and pot grower. Why pay for what you can grow or make yourself. When his Italian neighbours grassed him up, he built a twenty foot high brick wall down his forty foot garden; nice and shady.

Footslog Safari

One day I was sitting on the porch when a ruddy-faced Joshua turned up grinning and said "Hey, man, look what I've brought for you." A large cob of marijuana heads. Somehow we ended up at a boring dance at the old Nanuki Country Club. The only interesting guy there was called Chris Blackwell. He invited us to visit the 'farm' he was managing in the far north.

We decided on a cross-country trek across the lower slopes of Mount Kenya – rather than up it, like everyone else. What an up-hill, down-dale trek that was. There were no proper routes. We trudged through squelchy tropical forests, emerged into grasslands with a far border of pine trees! Cutting through a forest of bamboo thickets the paths began to split and diverge and get lower and lower, catching on our rucksacks. The shape of the tunnels became barrel-shaped and we realised with dry throats that we were in a rhino run.

We survived and ended up camping next to a huge neglected, slightly wonky watchtower on the edge of furry fir tree forest, no doubt planted by the Ministry of Agriculture and Forestry way back in the days of the Raj. Despite the squelchy undergrowth we had found no water so in a moment of inspiration I staked out my American army poncho (courtesy of Kaiserslautern) with a Billy can under the head opening. In the morning we had a nice Billy full of water for our morning tea. We followed forestry tracks, got a ride with some English squaddies on manoevres and ended up in a tiny woodland community with a huge log cabin, bar cum shop with virtually nothing for sale except beer.

We walked about the surrounding country which was tropical merging with the mountain pine and discovered an old deserted tree-tops hotel-type wooden structure overlooking a water hole that seemed to be half a mile below. We didn't linger as the structure started creaking. I've heard tell that a fruity Princess Elizabeth had spent part of her honeymoon in a similar spot.

We trekked back to the village over the fresh spoor of a large cat, probably a leopard, more scared of us than us of him. We took an afternoon nap and were woken by an ugly thud outside of the tent. A dead black and white monkey was lying there, eyes glazed, teeth bared. A young lad we had chatted to earlier was grinning through the tent flap.

"Look, bwana, I have brought you a monkey."

"Thanks, but no thanks." We made tea and chatted with the intelligent boy who was so pleased to practise his English on us.

En route with Chris to our rendezvous we made out way across another semi-desert of more millions of acacia trees. We stopped overnight with an old Danish dude who gave us a lift. His Kenyan missus/housekeeper treated us to a feast of food and he showed us an old picture of him astride a combination motorbike. I wonder if he was an old mate of Karen *Out of Africa* Blixen's?

The following day we arrived at the lonesome farmstead of an English couple, he a retired and tired naval officer. His still young -at-heart wife treated us handsomely and showed us to a two-bunk cabin.

"I think it's all tidy. We had William Thissiger and a couple of his dirty Arabs here last week." Sleeping in the footsteps of our hero!

Chris met us in his Land Rover and took us on a tour of his farm, another million acres of acacia semi-desert. Cleverly situated pumping stations fed giant circular green water tanks for the skinny cattle. In the midst of it all a well-watered small valley housed the eighty-year-old's house, cattle sheds and a tannery run by a blind Kenyan. I bought a half dozen beautifully soft sheepskins and some naturally tanned cowhide from which I would later make American Apache moccasins in London.

His own house was single storey, settler-style on a hill. His wife was an auburn-haired American beauty who was difficult to look at with out hungry, desert-trekking eyes. The next day she elected to take us out riding. She had an auburn-haired horse as beautiful and physically perfect as herself.

"Can either of you ride?" I raised my hand, thinking of old, plodding Papaw. I got a frisky grey Somalia pony. We wended our way through spiky, dangerous acacia bushes and came to a long straight red dirt road. She set off at a canter and I stood up in the saddle to follow and my cheeky little beast stopped dead in his tracks. I went straight over the top and ended up standing with the reins in my hand.

We cantered on, careering between razor-sharp bushes. Josh lolloping about in the saddle and me gripping for dear life. Our

American hostess rode her horse with the sickening style of a born horsewoman.

Our last adventure was to head north towards the Somalian border. In Kenya's northernmost town I danced, or should I say rhythmically jumped with a posse of Samburu women and demonstrated my knife-throwing skills to their delight. In the woodshack town we drank copious cups of wonderful smoked tea made with goat's milk and ogled the gorgeous Somali women. Masai warriors stood about leaning on spears doing nothing but looking beautiful with their long red ochre buttered locks and napkin rings of ivory lodged in their extended ear lobes.

I met some tribesmen with bows and arrows to sell. They came to our camp and demonstrated their erratic marksmanship, aiming a bevy of arrows at a fruit set in a big boled tree and missed by a mile. Josh and I tried a more successful and leisurely Robin Hood style.

Armed with three bows, a Bowie knife, a rucksack full of sheep skins, Josh and I set off to cross a section of white, uncharted territory on the Bartholemew's map. This in theory would bring us to a trading post on a barely used road south to connect with my plane in four days' time. We stopped briefly at a cluster of acacia thorn huts showing a lot of light through their sketchy roofs. Crossing through yet more acacia land we were calculating escape if attacked. There was not much chance of climbing up 5' high spiky thorn bushes, or of effective defence with the bundle of bows strapped to my rucksack.

A herd of thirsty cattle passed us with two small boys so we felt a bit safer. A couple of hours later, very hot and still surrounded by endless acacia, we were having an argument about a ten degree variation in where we thought our destination might be. Suddenly standing as still as a rock and silent as a tree we saw a lone Masai warrior with two spears in hand watching us. By some miracle of linguistics we were able to communicate and he pointed in the direction we had already decided on.

The two spears the Masai carry are to fight elephants with. There are two in case the warrior misses with the first!

We arrived, gasping from thirst at the road not marked on the map – no trading station in sight. We decided to go right and within 100 yards found a huge, almost dry waterhole with hundreds of animal footprints all around. It was obviously the site of the trading station from 30 years before. We went back up the road and found a

Samburu village of mud huts with spiky roofs. A Land Rover was parked there and an Italian priest in civvies wearing a dusty trilby greeted us. The Samburu were his flock. He treated us to the only meal of pasta in several million square miles!

He had once been a communist engineer and had converted to Christianity and ended up in Africa. He was a happy fellow and luckily for us, the only traffic on the supposed road. We had to wait a day for him to make a move and rode through herds of giraffe nibbling acacia buds to the nearest town. We arrived back at Ma Keneally's and she lent me her beat-up VW Beetle to go and visit the American lass up the mountain track to say goodbye. We had a farewell couple of glasses of whisky and I left jokingly saying, "I'm off to crash the car now."

The back end engine of the VW gives it a bad reputation for cornering. The road had been recently graded and the verges were loose shingle. As I floated too fast round a long bend the back wheel hit the soft and the car did a neat slow motion flip onto its roof. 30 years of Ma Keneally's tat and clobber showered down in the same slow motion as my metabolism tried to readjust to the upside-down, reversal of my journey. I was supposed to be flying home in two days! I staggered back to Mrs K's and Birmingham John came in the Land Rover with Josh. We righted the old grey Volkswagen. John punched out the roof dents, and made me drive it home.

It was sad leaving Mrs K. She was relaxed about the car. She had been a wise mentor to me and the months I spent with her was a gift from the Gods/Goddesses. Five years later I met someone in Sri Lanka who had just flown from Kenya and had stayed with her. She was still going strong into her 80s. I wrote her a long letter and got a lovely reply.

John decided to get me to the plane on time. We drove to Nairobi and camped overnight in City Park. We got ourselves completely wasted on some very good Malawi grass and staggered out of bed a bit late for the plane. John drove like a mini-minor jockey through the rush hour in his chunky Land Rover. We reached an out-of-town spot with a view of a flat green horizon. A jumbo jet lumbered into view. I was about to get on my first ever jet plane. We were arguing about whether it was taking off or landing with our hangover heads when it crashed in a napalm cascade of smoke and fire spread across the horizon.

It was the world's first jumbo jet crash. People in the forward part of the plane survived but a lot more died. As we entered the airport I saw two children, two parents and one grandparent dragging muddy bags across the airport concourse. I loaded my excessive luggage of animal skins, bows and arrows, Kenyan coffee etc. on the scales with my foot jammed under it. I went straight to the post office and sent my Mum a telegram saying I was OK!

She was standing at her window down the cobbled lane next to Pickford's warehouse in Highbury thinking about me. The news came on with a report of a plane crash in Nairobi. Simultaneously a telegraph boy arrived at the gate. In those days, telegrams meant two things, good news, or bad. With two sons dead already she got the wrong message and fainted, poor woman!

Months later back in England I went to the tiny sub post office in Stoke Newington wedged between a launderette and a baker's to post some tapes to Joshua in Kenya. The Indian postmaster looked at the address. "Kenya? My father used to be the station-master at Naro Maro near Mount Kenya!" Mrs Keneally once said of the messed-up days-late train service to Nairobi, "You used to be able to set your watch by the trains at Naro Muru when the Indian station-master was there."

Two years later my girlfriend would go to New York and visit an office on the umpteenth floor of a skyscraper. The next day she rang Joshua who was working in New York to arrange a meeting. He was working on the next floor up! Shrinking planet, and that was before mobiles and the internet.

1974: Drop-Out

My trip to the Yemen and Kenya had been magical. Far from being murdered, mugged or mutilated I had a charmed journey, hiding from hospitality, devouring distance on the Bartholemew map of the world. My travels amongst Muslim people in particular had given me a new perspective on humanity. My journey across the Sudanese desert with the generous dope-smoking trucker had shamed me. Here was I full of my pan-world socialist ideology and I couldn't even drive. A lot of us post university idealist travellers were the same, imbued with that essentially post-imperialist upper class, charitable outlook that said, "Oh, the poor 'natives!'"

The difference between us and the operatives of the old Empire that we despised was that we were in practical terms pretty useless with our book-heavy education.

My plan, inspired by my travels, was to buy a truck, drive it to India, sell it and buy a house in the cool, calm countryside with the proceeds. It sounds far-fetched, but people were still buying houses in Wales or rural Gloucestershire for £1,000-£3,000 in those days. I was just about to enter into a 25-year spell of careering about the planet and embarking on a new round of reality therapy. The difference was that I would be my own boss and would not pay a penny in income tax for another 20 years! And I would end up with my own house in the cool, calm countryside but not in the UK.

The first stage to becoming a trucker was to get a driving licence. I had applied for my driving test while I was still in Kenya so I wouldn't have to wait ages for it. I had already failed it twice despite driving the youth club minibus all around London and the sticks and Mrs K's car in Kenya. I went for my lesson with a chirpy Cockney in Leytonstone. After ten minutes he said, "Stop the car." He looked at me and said, "You can drive, can't you?"

"Yes."

"Well, why aren't you fucking well driving, then?"

"Er, because I'm trying to do it the way the examiner wants me to."

"That's my job. You just drive the car normally and I'll tell you where you are going wrong, OK?" Very OK. I passed three weeks later and have been driving for a living on and off for 25 years.

The next job was to get some work to earn the money to buy the truck. I had been staying at 9, Clissold Road, back in my old community of Karma cowboys/girls in Stoke Newington. I heard from someone who was down from our 'annexe' in Corwen, North Wales that there was an old school bus for sale up there and there was work on a big dam construction project.

I hitch hiked up the old A5 and went to stay at the Mill at Clwyd with Peter, Linda, Helen and the kids. I went up to the Massif Dam site ten miles up the road. The entire breadth of a valley was being filled with rock and rubble to form a natural dam without concrete. It needed to be double thick so hundreds of lorries were rushing about dropping puny loads. In the factory canteen full of big muddy geezers I got a contact for one of the contractors, Flockton's from Huddersfield. I found the foreman driver and his lads in a local pub.

"Looking for work, lad? Can ya drive lorry?"

"Oh yes," I lied, "I've been driving Land Rovers in Africa" - from the back seat. I turned up the next day for a test drive in a single cab, 20 ton yellow Tonka truck. A crash gearbox means no synchromesh and there's a technique called double de-clutching. It's a bit like riding a bike or skating. It's a question of co-ordination that, once learnt, is as easy as walking, but like walking, cycling, skating, there's a lot of crashing involved first. I went out with the lead driver crammed on the footplate of the tiny cab. We struggled up past a giant quarry on the edge of the site as I bungled the gear change, crashing about the box the truck veered towards the quarry's edge. Matey was half way out of the cab before I righted the vehicle.

By some miracle they took me on, for the night shift. It was a nightmare stuck in the muddy cab crashing the gears, queuing to get filled by an oversized digger, racing to the dam top, dumping and spreading the load, racing back for a refill, getting lapped by the piss-taking lads from Flockton's; talk about *Hell Drivers*.

Life at the Mill was generous. I handed over much needed cash and got fed, watered and woken. A handful of fellow 'freaks' working on the site made it tolerable. In my fourth week I was just about keeping up with the Flocktons, flying along the rocky road, racing to keep my place in the queue as I passed one of our lorries. A hail of rocks spun off my back wheels and one of them, the size of a grape-fruit went straight through the window of the truck behind, whizzed past the driver's ear and out through the rear window. Alan the boss called me in and gave me the sack.

"Sorry lad, but you nearly killed one of the Flockton's boys tonight." What a relief! I'd saved enough cash to buy my own lorry!

The pretty old bus in the Corwen car park was a classic but impracticable as it had a petrol engine. I hitched back to Clissold Cloisters.

(2004) I recently met some lads from Huddersfield and asked them about Flocktons. I always thought it was named after the boss. It is actually named after a place that used to have the record for the highest number of road deaths in Yorkshire. Why? Because the pub closed at 11 and all the others closed at 10.30. All the piss-up lads in Yorkshire would race over for last orders and get 'smashed' on the way; Hell Drivers *mark 2.*

(2005) Rolling over the hills towards Huddersfield and Hebden Bridge on a sunlit afternoon I happened across tiny Flockton village. Turning into the pub car park I spotted a bald-headed geezer standing next to his mechanic's van. "'Scuse me, mate, d'you know Flockton Transport?"

"Should do, lad, used to drive for them."

"Are they still about?"

"You're lucky, lad, they've sold up and closed down but the governor's up in't yard havin' a last clear-up." I told him I'd written a book with Flockton Transport in it. He laughed.

"Would you like me to give him a call for you?" he said, pulling out his mobile phone.

"Hello, Paul. It's Paul. I've got a bloke called Paul 'ere wants to talk to you about a book."

I drove up to the yard. The series of well-worn, giant corrugated sheds stood on a deserted apron of asphalt. A big, blonde, weather-faced bloke in scuffed tan leather work boots with steel toe caps was sweeping the already clean yard. I introduced myself and told him how he was responsible for all of my subsequent four and six-wheeled perambulations about the Planet by giving me my first driving job and the wherewithal to buy my first truck. He liked the story and some of the anecdotes I told him. Like a thousand and one other businesses of the old school with organic roots in people and place, he was closing up and selling the land to the property developers to build million-pound pads on the rolling Yorkshire hills.

He told me the real story of Flockton, now the home of the North Yorkshire Mining Museum occupying the old mine site. Flockton's had been

173

contracted to the National Coal Board, shifting millions of tons about the country and had died a slow death since the 1974 miner's strike. The pit workers would finish at ten o'clock and had half an hour to clean up after their shift. The two local pubs had a special dispensation till eleven so they could get a drink. The problem was, as the only pubs in Yorkshire with a late licence it got to the point where the miners couldn't get through the door any more.

I had a few A4 bound copies with me so I offered him one for a tenner, explaining that they actually cost me £11.50. As I reached into my bag he grinned, held onto his tenner quite tightly and said "You sure you haven't got a bloody suitcase full of these in there, lad?" I prised the tenner out of his large hand. I said, "You'll be paying the full price, you bloody Yorkshireman" and duly signed and dedicated it to him and his family.

1974: ALLY PALLY AUCTIONS

A couple of American hippy hill-billies were hanging out in Clissold Road in a home-made German Hanomag camper. They agreed to take me to the auctions. In those good old days all the public utilities, water, gas, electric, phones and post were still owned by us the people, all part of the Welfare State fought and voted for by the millions of Brits who had gone to war, 1939-1945. Trucks and vans, mostly old British Leylands, built like battleships, were regularly sold off at auctions. The British work ethic, in those far-off days was about service, quality and jobs for everyone. After all, everyone was expected to fight or produce stuff to fight with during war time, so it was only fair play that everyone had a job even if they didn't do too much, or serviced trucks that didn't need servicing, in peace time!

Alexandra Palace auction in North London was stuffed with strange workshop motors, armoured Post Office vans and all sorts of utility vehicles, most of which didn't have much value in the second hand truck trade. Dealers bought at knock-down prices to cut them for scrap or sell on. Self-employed builders and oppos bought cheap motors in pillar box red from the Post Office or daffodil yellow from the GPO (telephones). Sitting like two ugly ducklings were two turd-brown BMC FG GPO workshop trucks with a 10' x 7' x 7' box and a six-seater crew cab with fold-down tea-table. Made for cable-laying and general hole digging duties, they spent most of their working lives standing still while their crews did what was on the worksheet and spent the rest of the day drinking tea.

Next to the two turds stood another identical truck with its box built in bright mottled aluminium, looking like a giant camera case! The American boys kicked the wheels and said, "Look's like a solid rig to me, Goodsie." How did they know? Did their Grandads drive stage-coaches and every day check their spoked wheels by giving them a kick? I don't know, but I've seen hundreds of people do it. Maybe we were all wheelwrights or coachmen once upon a time and wheel-kicking is in our genes?

Three guys in flashy nylon jackets were standing around.

"Thinking of buying that motor, boys?"

"Yes," I said in my best imitation hard man voice.

"Well, so are we, so it's going to get expensive."

"Well, I'm still bidding." One of them wearing glasses took me to one side. "Look, mate, we've got a Mini racing team and that's the perfect motor for us. If you want to stay out of the bidding I'll bung you £20."

"OK, I'll think about it."

The first turd went through for £55 + VAT. The aluminium box came next. I kept my hand down. It went for £55, too. The second turd came up and I bid it to £55 against some dealers. £67-50 including VAT, but I only had £50. I'd only gone for a look. Bugger!

The auctioneer called me over to pay. I made a quick détour and found Mini-man. He bunged me the £20 and I was the proud owner of the first of what was to become about 150 lorries. I had £2.50 change to stick some diesel in, but then it was 1979 and I could put 10 gallons in for that money!

It's funny, but once you've got a lorry everyone wants something moving. Driving a mini-lorry with a crash box was a doddle after my stint as a Hell Driver in Wales.

My first ever job was taking a Nigerian band called the Funkees to a gig in the West End. We spluttered to a halt at the top of Holloway Hill on the way home and the boys pushed me over the top. One of the Action House kids' parents, young Jackie Patterson's, in fact, had an antique shop. They gave me some furniture moves to do. I discovered I had an uncanny sense of direction in London. On my first ever drop I pictured the address in St John's Wood and it was exactly right. Years later this sense of direction would nearly get me killed in Amsterdam.

Another scam was selling second hand bricks. Lenny and I knocked down a wall at the back of our old adventure playground. The smog-brown London stocks were held apart rather than together with a lime mortar/horsehair mix and perfect Flemish bonding. The reverse sides were a beautiful crunchy bar honeycomb colour. Every time I drive through Canonbury Square and certain other parts of London I can see slightly yellower than normal walls built with my bricks.

One time I was loading 3,000 bricks onto a scaffold set on a concrete basement. I was standing on the scaffold boards loading the last few hundred bricks into a small gap in what was a brick mountain. Behind me was a low garden wall where the bricks were being placed for me. There was a sickening lurch as one of the scaffold legs drove through the cheap, thin concrete skin. I swear that Tai Chi, the slow-motion martial art, saved my life. I turned ever so harmoniously, placed two hands behind on the garden parapet and eased myself, slowly as a floating feather, up on out of the man-sized gap as 3,000 bricks crashed into the basement.

Scrap metal was another caper. Emptying out old sewing machine workshops, sorting out piles of copper pipes, brass taps, lead flashings into their appropriate piles and weighing them in at a tiny scrapyard in Hornsey. Gypsies, builders, Greeks, Cypriots, Jamaicans, Irish travellers were the regular customers. We were the first hippies at it. There was a curious camaraderie. We were all outsiders and we got taught the rules and language of the game by dirty-faced, bright-eyed geezers. The scrapyard boss once asked me who I reckoned was the wealthiest people in the country in terms of cash.

"The Jews?"

"No, the Gypsies. Someone lost £30,000 in cash from his caravan last week."

One of the best things about my new occupation was driving around London with a massive TV windscreen of humanity in front of me.

SIMBA THE DOG

I had acquired a dog a few months before. I had been in Wales, saw some Labrador pups and said, "I wouldn't mind one of those." A couple of weeks later a lass called Jane turned up with two pups, one for her, one for me! He was a tiny baby-face thing with floppy feet. I took him for a walk up to the park with a piece of string round his neck. As I got to the zebra crossing I went to walk across and the hound sat down. We seemed to get on really well so I kept him and called him Simba which means 'lion' in Swahili. His boss trick, once he'd grown a bit was following me around town on my old GPO push bike.

The old BMC FG lorries I drove had tiny windows on their front corners and Simba would curl up in front of the passenger seat and watch where we were going. I was always stopping off at friends' houses across London and or knocking on front doors and asking people if they wanted the old bike, bath or whatever in their front garden. Simba was so used to us making ourselves at home here and there that he would often walk into some complete stranger's homes and settle down.

Part of the point of having a lorry was to give me mobility and I was always looking for an opportunity to get out into the sticks. In the mid '70s there was a big movement of people out of the cities to the rustic margins. Wales, with more of its population living in London than in Wales, was a favourite destination, but all remote parts of the UK were being resettled. Also a lot of ex-students, as in the English East Coast scene, were staying on in under-populated rural towns, provincial cities and creating New Age rustic retreats.

A big part of the post dope cultural revolution was that people were buying up cheap houses, renovating, altering, amending and building in a variety of different and creative styles. Recycling was born; Victorian fireplaces and doors that were being trashed ten years before were being renovated and reinstalled in place of 50s and 60s modernity. The alternative food business grew too. The new breed of eco-immigrants didn't want to eat supermarket food. They wanted muesli, brown rice, honey, seaweed, etc.

My old pal Andrew Jedwell from Clissold Road, who I had started a food co-op with before going to Yemen started a wholefood business in his bedroom above the milliners' shop in Corwen. When he asked his bank manager for a loan to rent the shop next door the manager replied, "Oh, good – I won't have to go to Shrewsbury for my muesli any more." Today Jedwell's/Meridan foods is one of the biggest suppliers of wholefoods in Wales with several of its own brands on the markets and is the supplier of Dorito Dips. Andrew still lives in his Welsh rustic retreat.

To the south Llandridnod Wells and Builth Wells were the centres of an invasion of eco-immigrants. I was asked by a character called Van to take a load of wholefoods back up to Wales. He was a retired dealer from London who was renting a ramshackle farm house and a shop on the edge of town, for £2 a week.

All of these hippy wholefood shops acted as information/marriage bureaux, hitchhikers' bus stations, job centres for the burgeoning population of 'freaks', hippies, drop-outs, whatever the collective identity might be. I accepted Van's offer and drove down to London to load up at Community Supplies. This was situated in an old squatted bakery in Kentish Town and run by a guy called John Law.

Across the road a guy called Catweazle* was running London's first genuine 100% wholewheat bakery. For those of us reared on the whiter-then-white wonders of Wonderloaf it was a liberation of the taste buds. This was the beginings of the British wholefood and Organic movement that like everything else is being aped by the supermarket chains often putting the pioneers out of business.

* *Catweazle died in Bristol recently, where he was a member of the anarchist collective Kebele Cafe, another ex-squat. He was such an eco-warrior that he had once ridden his bicycle to the Sierra Nevada in Spain. His fellow co-op members took his coffin to burial on his beloved bicycle.*

I decided to take my Mum along for her first trip to Wales in forty years, since running away with my Dad at seventeen. She used to go on trips away with Billy Miller when they first met so he agreed.

Roy Harper once wrote a song called 'Pity the White Immigrant' which struck a chord with me. Like Asian, Indian, Caribbean folk in the fifties and sixties, in the thirties and forties English, Welsh, Irish and Scottish folk were still migrating to the cities in an ongoing continuum of the Industrial Revolution. 'Community' became a big

buzzword in the sixties precisely because old working class communities based around occupation (dockers, printers, miners) etc. were
disappearing. Any stranger to a big town is an immigrant white,
black or brown.

How much time is there outside of work to create communities
that are not based on pub or football club culture? Religion was very
much on the decline so no longer fulfilled that social function. Once a
city/council estate/family like mine became dysfunctonal through
divorce or death and moved house because of change of work, we
became foreigners in our own land, rootless, often propertyless and
with a low or semi-skilled occupational status. In so many ways being
the product of a series of broken homes, student of 13 different
schools, itinerant citizen of umpteen different towns; I was the white
immigrant, the man from nowhere.

African, Asian, Greek etc. immigrants have the distinct advantage
of their race, religion and common culture. Dysfunctional or alienated
indigenous individuals cannot achieve the same degree of
community or social cohesion. It is the reason why so many white,
middle class people are attracted to exotic cultures; because of their
own lack of social cohesion. It is also one of the root causes of
working class racism, the cultural takeover of areas, particularly
those of declining industrial importance (e.g. Blackburn) whose
communal identity was based, not on religion, race or belief, but often
on a single industry work based culture.

The post sixties culture revolution had sex 'n drugs 'n rock 'n roll
and revolution as its unifying factor. People popping round to score
was just the same as visiting the general store in pre-supermarket
days. The meeting places of live music venues and the shared identity
of afficionados of the rapidly changing music styles; all gave common
cause. Political movements and religious cults, the anti-war
movement, Socialist Workers, Hare Krishna, Buddhists, Sufis, all
created an alternative sense of community outside of a mainstream
culture where worship of God was being increasingly replaced by the
worship of Gelt.

As a déclassé person with no roots or vocational skills, I was at
the same time completely free and absolutely alone. Luckily being a
Sagittarian means that the horizon is my one point of reference and
being on the move twixt point A and point B is my true home. It was
essentially the same for hundreds of thousands of others; as Uncle

Bob Dylan quite rightly said, "The times they are a-changing."

It had started in the sixties and was consolidating in the early-mid seventies into so many of the cultural phenomena that we have today and take for granted, and the BBC and their pals are only just catching up with. The new religions of travel, house makeovers, buying rustic retreats, doing Sunday worship at the organic/vegetarian food counter at Tesco's, or pilling it up with the trance-dance posse at the city centre clubs was part of an ongoing cultural revolution that had shared roots in the co-op movement, working class radicalism. anti war poets, socialist intelligentsia, the sacrifices of war, the advance of technology, equal rights etc., etc. All of it accelerated and trumpeted through millions of mouths and thousands of guitars in the heady sometimes, dope-inspired rush of the sixties and seventies.

This trip to Wales with my Mum was a double opportunity for us both, the sole survivors of a once large family unit. The difference was that my post-hippy identification with the forces of the cultural revolution gave me an ability to feel at home wherever I might be. There was always bound to be a fellow traveller, dope smoker, muesli-muncher, Buddhist trucker somewhere, particularly in rural Wales. Me and Mum were about to visit our real roots.

The trip to Wales was hilarious. The truck was completely overloaded. Van had spent more on food than he had in the bank. He had smashed up a hire van on his previous trip. Mum prattled on non-stop like a bird released from its cage. On top of that I had teamed up with a gorgeous red-haired American girl, Angélique who was so spaced out on LSD that she had left part of her mind in orbit, but she did get on with my Mum who, after all, had danced with Douglas Fairbanks Jr. and knew how to wrestle the djinns from the bottom of a gin bottle.

By the time we had bumped up to Van's farmhouse up a very rocky buggered-up drive, the sub-frame of the crew cab of my lovely lorry had dropped. Mum immediately started to right the semi-submerged wreck of a communal dope smokers' country farm house sinking under a welter of washing-up and friendly filth. Somehow we squeezed the contents of the truck into Van's tiny shop and set off south to find my Mum's old stamping ground not far from Oswestry.

Van is now joint biggest supplier of wholefoods in Wales with Andrew Jedwell and has a small fleet of 40 ton lorries – not bad for a retired dealer.

We stopped at a country pub and a sleek, grey-haired Errol Flynn lookalike excused himself at the door as he left. It turned out that he was one of my Mum's old suitors. We got invited to stay over with some friendly freaks – as one did in those days. The next day we found The Lion at Llanbuflin where my Mum had swept water out of the basement just before some prospective purchasers turned up. We finished our trip at the Red Lion at Llanmanarch with its front in England and back in Wales. It still had three little stone steps in the yard where the ladies of the local hunt would mount side-saddle.

We meandered happily back to London down the A40 and I managed to sell the truck to the Pattersons for the same money I had bought it for. I went straight out to an auction in Leighton Buzzard and bought another identical truck.

1975: MOVING MOUNTAINS

BOURG ST MAURICE

Colin Dixon, my revolutionary vet friend had run away with the French doctor's wife from the Yemen. He had settled in the high Alps of Haute Savoie near the border with Italy above a town called Bourg St Maurice. I met him at the flat he sometimes shared with his sister in Stoke Newington. The kitchen doubled up as a bathroom and he had a Welsh Alpine billy goat with horns sitting in the bath with a sack sowed up to its neck and doped up on something. He was about to drive back down with Dominique, her son Mathieu and the goat in a 2CV! He invited me to travel over, bring some stuff for him and his cousin and a friend.

After Colin's introduction to the Yemen I was ready for another break from the round of dope-smoking fantasies and being a part time scrap metal man. I had met up with another American lass, Gay, who knew how to eat well, smoke dope without tobacco and could speak French. Colin's mission was to make a viable, self-sufficient lifestyle in the mountains. He had a head start on all the other eco-immigrants because he was an animal smuggling vet, which was quite handy in the cool, calm countryside. He was also a genuine truth-seeker with a library of esoteric literature from the Bhagavad Gita through to Gurdjieff and Ouspensky. He had an impatient attitude to people and someone once said that he only became a vet rather than a doctor because he couldn't get on with people. Nevertheless he was always inviting others along on what for most of us would be life changing missions.

The village of Vulmix was a lengthy wind up the mountains of Haute Savoie on the middle slopes of the Alps. A settlement of only ten houses or so, most of them unoccupied holiday homes. The meadows about were a fiesta of flowers and tall grass ringed with ripe cherry trees. The style of the houses were original mountain chalet, built from massive boulders and rough cut timber.

Colin's roof was in trouble, a rafter was gone. The apex was a big tree trunk, the rafters smaller tree trunks, the slates 3' wide and 3" thick. Colin's solution was to jack the broken timber with a car jack, insert another alongside it and the two of us whack it home with sledge hammers, whilst perched on the terrace. It actually worked, but he wouldn't let me cut the end clean because he considered doing things for appearance only was a bourgeois luxury.

I got some work delivering timber to the highest villages. The road was so steep I rested the truck halfway. Colin, who was also a master mechanic/participant in the Barcelona Motorcycle Grand Prix, laughed. "I wish I was your truck, to be so pampered!"

A laughing old lady met us on one trip and said she loved living in the company of eagles. Two German dudes turned up in an outlandish mini-truck they had made from a VW beetle chassis. Another trip took me high, high up to a rustic paradise of falling water with a view for hundreds of miles with a group of earnest Christians determined to return to the land.

Gay and I travelled back to England alone and Colin gave us a parting gift of some of his home-grown dope. On the way south we had passed a mirage – I was driving through the French countryside, ripe with wheat and bursting sunflowers when I glimpsed a bushy green field. I looked again and then again in disbelief. It was a plantation of massive dope plants. I crept in and chopped off some branches. We had dried and smoked some and although it wasn't mega-weed it did do something. The plan was to pick some, dry it and flog it to finance the journey home. What we had actually found was commercial hemp grown for paper, fibre and animal food

We arrived at dawn. Grey/white Charolais cattle floated ghost-like in the morning mist. Clutching my old Bowie knife between my teeth I clomped through the sodden clay field, feet getting bigger by the step, heart pumping with paranoia at the thought of being sussed out by an angry French farmer.

Funny thing, karma, it really does work, in the negative and positive.

We only got a few miles down the road and the vehicle spluttered, jerked and staggered along for a few miles and conked out in the midst of a hot prairie of wheat fields, ameliorated only by Napoleon's tree-shaded roads. I spent the day stripping out the diesel system and caught a fever. I had to lie down in a tiny stone hut for a couple of hours and sleep it off. All the next day I toiled away until I gave up and walked to the nearest town. A friendly mechanic with a barn full of old motors and tractors came out and towed us to his workshop. It was late and they invited us to supper and let us sleep in the truck in the garage.

It was so good to get a proper meal after being stuck for two days in the hot wheatbowl of central France. I think the family were Spanish and being immigrants themselves, looked after us with the understanding of immigrants. They knew we were skint. The next day the son rapidly stripped out my lift pump and found a worn out Woodruff key a tiny half moon of metal, delved in his tractor mender's box and fitted a new one in the space of an hour. That tiny half-moon of metal had been enough to prevent fuel distribution and had sabotaged the three tons of vehicle. I went down to the cool of the village washrooms and knocked up a couple of leather belts, one for the dad, one for the son. We motored on towards Paris, the marijuana drying on the roof.

We hung around for days trying mostly unsuccessfully to sell some of our hemp/grass; at very fair prices I have to say. Gay hit on the idea of hanging out at American Express and trying to find some riders back home who could help pay the way. In those days most adventurers used travellers' cheques and the American Express offices were the places to meet like-minded souls. The first person I met was a New York detective sergeant who was on a 6 month sabbatical. He was a very relaxed blonde haired guy with a Paul Newman look about him. He was trying to sell his VW Variant he had been travelling around Europe in. He was up for travelling with us back to the UK; if he could sell his car.

It was hard work finding riders so we hung out at the Gare du Nord where people would be getting trains for England. Eventually we gathered a motley crew, a horse-loving lass who could drive the truck, an Irish lad and two others. As we were leaving the station I spotted the American cop. He had already bought a ticket but he cashed it in and came with us. I've always had this knack of meeting up with switched-on policemen or members of the military. For many a working class truth-seeker the only way to break out of the constrictions of their environment is to join the military or Police, just like I had once tried to join the RAF to see the world and earn a living.

We booked onto the new hovercraft to Ramsgate. As soon as we rolled off the ramp we were stopped by a female customs officer. In those days they would get all the lasses who had been taken on as glorified VAT clerks out of their offices in the summer and train them up as good old contrabandista busters. The trouble is they were too keen to prove themselves in a man's world and therefore were an overzealous nuisance. I still had a good amount of marijuana hidden in a large Long Life beer tin stuffed with wild flowers on the dashboard. As our protagonist made me open the back door I noticed two guys wrapped in motorbike leathers waddling onto a big Italian bike like two mighty Michelin men who have something to hide. Luckily for them we were being turned over by the VAT keenies as they rode off. Later I would meet one of them in the middle of the night driving North on the cusp of my 28th birthday.

Mrs Vatwoman found a Queen Elizabeth Coronation tin in the back of the van with a couple of joint's worth of dope from Colin in it; we were busted again! Her boss, a wise, old school customs guy took us into the office.

"What's this?" he asked. "I believe it to be a class 'B' prohibited drug."

"I don't know, I've picked up so many hitchhikers, maybe someone left it in there," I lied.

"Well, on this occasion, we're going to throw it down the toilet," and he did just that and handed the tin back to me! Mrs Vatwoman looked really pissed off. I would meet her on two other occasions in the ensuing years but she never did get a result.

My American cop pal rejoined us, laughing.

"That was funny," he said. "They asked me if you were toking and smoking on the ferry. Of course, I told them that you were really straight guys." He came back to Stoke Newington and stayed in our street of semi-legal squats. Funny world. He reckoned some of his cops smoked but he didn't cos you needed to be super-fit chasing people down the street with stolen tellys!

The laughing policeman stayed in Clissold Cloisters for a week hob-nobbing genially with our tribe of antisocial dope heads and loved it.

LONDON: FULLY QUALIFIED SURVIVOR

DIRTY TRUCK DRIVER, WORKING FOR A FIVER.

Flushed with the success of my first PG Trips excursion to the Alps, I was also besotted with the organic stick and stone lifestyle of the mountain margins; Wales and France where houses were still cheap. A guy called Roger Dainton had bought a house in a Gloucestershire village for £1,000.

This became a financial target:. £1,000 = 1 house. I wanted to be a middle class hippy like everyone else but a) there was no wedge in the family and b) I was no good at selling dope, which was what some of the other people I knew were doing. Mr Marks and his pals were sewing the seeds of alternative Britain.

The sub-plot was to drive to India, sell my truck and buy a house in the cool, calm countryside with the proceeds. Crazy idea, but, in a long-winded, ham-fisted, contorted, chaotic and karmic way I achieved it, mostly thank to Colin Dixon, VS, bless his soul.

The major problem was cash! And skills to obtain it. School and university had left me with zero practical or professional skills. I was going to have to teach myself. There was no way I could earn a living in the countryside, and my nature is too generous to be a successful businessman.

Owning a love truck was a rite of passage. Six years in boarding school learning how to make a teapot stand in woodwork, never living anywhere and with no male role models/ teachers about meant I didn't even know the difference between a ball pane hammer and a metric or ASF spanner.

The one thing I didn't want was a proper job. I took a £2-a-week room in the legalised squat in Clissold Road. Martin Turner, meanwhile, had finished building a beautiful two-storey house on stilts with a half dome-cum-roof made up of coloured glass, plastics and wood. It was his answer to the American woodbutchers' cabins. Nestling under the trees in the back yard of No. 9, it was a work of living art and an example to the rest of us creative layabouts.

I was lucky enough to pick up bits of removal work, some building/advanced bodging work, trucking bands around and generally making myself useful; the dirty truck driver working for a fiver syndrome. I was slowly improving my quiver of skills and "street" knowledge. Luckily for me and my dream of living in the sticks a lot of other people were already doing it and I would get the job of shifting their stuff to funky, rustic destinations and over the next four years would evolve a lifestyle with one foot in the countryside and the other in London. I was determined not to spend the next forty years in London like my Mum, building up a base that I would never be able to leave.

The other thing that was guaranteed to nail the foot to the ground were the ladies and the bonnie babies. I was getting into my late twenties, and had a run of sexual relationships with mostly American lasses passing through but seemed to have gone beyond the frontiers of procreativity I had approached with the Maglet. There was a kind of hollowness to sex-only relationships and I was beginning to think I may never become a father. That notwithstanding and the fact that I had, and always have had, a debilitatingly romantic outlook that enables me to fall in love every other day, I still maintained a hope of meeting Ms Right.

Trouble is that the combination of smoking libido-enhancing hashish and pornographic presentation of women always confused sexuality, romance, fantasy, companionship, shared vision and procreation.

There was also the problem of the spiritual path. We'd smoked so much dope, lit enough joss sticks, fondled brass Buddhas for some of the essence of the East to rub off on us. Not to mention tea. The nearest the average Cockney gets to Oriental mystery is in his cup of "Rosie Lee".

My own rootless and dysfunctional background left me in a strange place. I was both free of all the attachments of family/place/occupation but in a search for all of these quite normal expectations, a phantom boat from nowhere afloat on an unknown ocean en route to an undefined somewhere.

The one certainty was that I was a dysfunctional mess and there was no point in indulging in promising eternal love and creating another human being until I had sorted myself out. Like so many others of my generation I maintained a fantasy of going to the East and finding a Guru to lead me to enlightenment, as well as flogging a motor and buying a pad in the cool, calm countryside. Neat plan, eh?

Another way of looking at this 'to procreate/ not procreate' conundrum is that we were the first generation who were lucky enough to have the luxury of staring into the abyss of self knowledge/delusion. Ultimately we had to become more self aware just by dint of practice. This would mean that our kids might be a bit further down the path to enlightenment as well. After all, the development of civilisation should be as much about the human mind and spirit as well as material progress. However it was that generous post war period of material advance that provided us with the time, space and facilities to pursue our dreams,the student grants, the £50 motors, £2 a week rooms, cheap grub, free medicine, the birth control pill etc. The hard bit was having to work it all out as we went along. There were no guidelines. The sages were dealing with history and our parents were to busy dealing with their own pasts. We were alone on the frontiers of change. No wonder we were making so many mistakes but, we were still the unwitting pioneers of a new epoch and we got some of it right and spread a few smiles around.

In practical terms our generation in some part effected an evolutionary slowing down of the rate of population increase. My mother and father had their first child at 16. I had mine at 32. I had skipped a generation. This delay in the biological clock is hard to deal with on an emotional or intellectual level and has contributed to the division of so many relationships. How long can two people go on making love without procreating and before negativity and mutual self-destruct sets in?

I have always found that after two years a sexual relationship starts to decline and self-destruct. My theory is that a sense of what the Buddhists call 'dissatisfaction' sets in, no matter how good the sexual satisfaction has been previously, because no procreation has occurred. Some couples can survive, through all sorts of reasons, conscious or practical. Many do not and fall off the wall of love and sometimes find it very hard to get back on.

When there was no particular work about I would meander across London, sometimes staying overnight with pals in Notting Hill Gate or South London. It was a kind of urban, itinerant existence. All my friends were seeker/creative types or community workers. This was the post 60s and many of my ex-student revolutionary pals were settling into switched-on and useful occupations: sculpture workshop, making music, teaching, care work etc. It was a burgeoning, creative community and I was always doing my best to introduce people to each other. I knew what a lonely place London could be. My theory was that the more people got to know each other the better it would be for everyone. If we were all mates, how could we wage war anymore? Naïve, eh?

The trouble with this community of like-minded people doing similar things with broadly matching beliefs was that the only unifying theme was me – a lot of them didn't actually know each other. I was the only unifying factor with my half-baked, post-revolutionary, pantheist ideology.

One of the big problems with Clissold Road and any gathering of people on the margins is that it usually attracts strong-minded individuals. Without any unifying principles, common cause or business to focus on, over and above hedonistic pursuits, political idealism or smoking dope, any community will eventually implode beyond the realms of friendship. The problem stemmed from the post-Protestant cult of the individual, all of the people who had escaped small-town Britain or the rigours of regular employment were highly independent survivors – a vague community of thought might exist, but communal action, no way!

When the denizens of Clissold Road housing co-op were given £1,000,000 by Ken Livingstone's GLC to refurbish the street nobody could agree on what to do or how to do it. The Street was full of builders and useful people but they couldn't communicate on a communal level. The community ended up employing an architect and 'normal' builders who did a sufficient job that nevertheless killed off some of the communal aspects of the large, airy-roomed Georgian houses. Everyone was so busy being individually free they voted themselves into being boxed into very separate apartments. With changing lives, growing kids and junkie neighbours, maybe it was a good thing.

One thing was for sure, the free pads and £2 rooms were gone. Rents were going up to a realistic price – and they would be tied to inflation in the future – no more Mr Nice Guy … but everyone would still be getting stoned. Mr Nice was still in business.

Wives and Wardrobes out the Window

I was doing one of my cross-town manoevres one day when I spotted a bunch of old awkward style wardrobes outside of a big bay-fronted Victorian house. I pulled up and shouted across the road to a character leaning out of the window.

"Oi, mate, d'you want to give me £20 to get rid of that lot?"

He turned round and said, "Yes please, Paul!" It was my old mate Johnny Roster, a guitarist who used to work with the kids in Peckham, teaching them guitar and doing jam sessions, he in turn was an old school friend of Martin's from Stoke. His best mate in their band Oxo-Whitney was a guy called Pete Ward. His girl friend was Claire Chamberlain, the granddaughter of the guy who had started the 2nd World War and ended up giving his job to Winston C. There he was again!

Anyway, this particular building was a squat. There were loads of them around London, houses that had been shut up years before owned by intestate families, local councils, developers waiting for money. Mostly they were in original Victorian condition with wonky toilets, sometimes outside, old gas geysers and, best of all, open fires. Small groups of mates would crack the houses and rapidly fill the rooms up, moving in furniture found on the street, or build it. Often whole streets that had been compulsorily purchased to build a new school or road would be hit, like Clissold Road.

It happened all across London in Brixton, Camden Town, Islington, Elephant and Castle. The core community would draw in others, particularly foreigners, French, German, Dutch, American, all passing through one of the world's cross-roads. My mate Franco from Amalfi speaks Napolitano and squatted in Finsbury Park for 10 years and learnt Italian by living with people from Rome and Milano! It was a uniquely classless, multicultural gathering of people. Food was often shared or cooked on a communal basis. Certain squats might be organised on well-defined socialist, anarchist or religious principles. It was an open-ended, trusting society where everyone could get by and start to build futures. The low rents and costs allowed people the time to invest in creative pursuits or new futures.

Many a squat-based band has made it big, writers, poets, artists have been nurtured and all sorts of contributions to society made; and the parties were great!!

This squat in Beresford Road was new and peopled with creatives and boy builders. There was Sexy Micky the Slow-Motion Electrician, live wire Sheelagh, Johnny's girl friend and a couple of her friends plus Dave Green, a 'real' Londoner who was roadie to a soul band and drove a green Jaguar 240.

I went on up to the top of the house and a girl was painting the outline of a corseted lady on a red wall, an exact copy of the same figure painted on a mirror. It was sort of cross-over Andy Warhol/Surrealist. The rest of the room was a mess. It was in the worst condition of all of them.

I offered to help and rolled up the old-school '50s printed lino underlaid with dusty sheets of the *News of the World*. I looked out of the window and shouted "Below!" and lobbed the whole lot onto the pavement two storeys below, followed by other deconstructed bits of furniture.

I was impressed by a sense of selflessness about the person I had just met – occupying the crappest room in the house but more interested in painting a mural on the wall than creating creature comfort. We would know each other for the rest of our lives. Our relationship started a few weeks later after I bought a bottle of Glenfiddich to take to a party in south London. It was such a raucous do she nearly jived somebody out of the window. We ended up the two last lost souls of the party and I could still drive. The rest is a history that took a long while to get properly started.

Apart from the mutual admiration society and lots of laughter, early on the thing that I realised about this person was that in an unstated ways here was someone who was in exactly the spiritual place/space I aspired to. How long was it going to take for me to get there? I wasn't sure, but I still had to give it a go. When driving a heavy old diesel truck around London all day, or grovelling in a pile of scrap metal, a carrot on a stick is needed to provide illumination at the end of the tunnel and I was determined to give it a try. I had to go to India to find myself and in a way I did, but not in the way I planned. Mother India is a great destroyer of illusion. I would return not as new age Saddhu but with a wife and child.

She was an accomplished designer and worked producing designs on recycled card. It was called ReGenesis and must have been one of the first companies in its genre, a typical example of a small two-person beginning becoming a multi-million pound business, but without the pioneers on board.

She came from a literary family and for the first time I met people of what I call the aristocracy of the mind. There was a fairly well known uncle who was a writer and poet who lived in Majorca. Having got bored to tears with 'A' level English Lit. and failed my exams after my early promise with the English language, I didn't have a clue who he was and had him confused with Somerset Maugham, who also lived in the Med!!

Despite our closeness I had to hit the trail again. London was my piggy bank but it wasn't my yard. I had to head off for the horizon and I got a load taking some stuff up to mid Wales for a couple of London-based ex-student friends of friends. They had bought a very marginal smallholding on the edge of sheep-grazing country. The previous owners had lived and survived on the meagre agricultural margins.

There was a small dairy annexe and I was touched by the time- and hand-worn stone surfaces of the cleaning area. There was a century-old wholesome cleanliness to the room that reached right down into the rock. It like the Spice Road had been polished by human toil and hand on heart in a way that machines can never replicate.

I detoured home via Tim and Lis Cutting's farm in Herefordshire. In another one of those mind-bending co-incidences that have touched my life, Henry Williamson's "Gypsy" caravan, where he had written *Tarka the Otter* was parked under a giant walnut tree, sharing a paddock with a friendly piggy! Jackie Gallard had worked with him, editing the same book. The literary connections were piling up and I had already started writing poems on the backs of fag packets in between all my other blunderings about the planet.

Life in Herefordshire with Tim and the Mackintosh toffee heiress and their well-to-do mates who could afford their drop-out lifestyles was idyllic, but penniless Paul had to head home to the Smoke and sort out his destiny.

STOKE NEWINGTON TOWN

HIGH ROADS AND BLACK SHADOWS

Life on the margins of London was losing its lustre for me. The happy hashish highs were degenerating into a hedonistic rut of low grade cocaine use, mediocre music and a loss of the community vibe we had started with. I was yearning for the hills and I knew any move towards getting a "proper" job or going back to community work meant putting down deeper roots in London that would keep me there for another decade or two. Getting serious in the city meant getting a decent pad, forming a lasting relationship, or at least giving it a go. These were all material illusions in my Quasi-Buddhist/Hindu view of life. It was time to move on.

Lisa, the lass who had worked at the youth club with us was working at a Rudolph Steiner school in Aberdeen, Scotland so I decided to pack all my collected junk together and go to Scotland. It was early November so not only was I looking for the light but it was starting to get dark, especially in Scotland. The recurring theme of my wandering life is one of having unexpected magical meetings and life-shaping coincidences. I have probably created a few for other people too, along the way. I can think of several marriages and children born to mutual friends I introduced, for a start! My lonely journey north up the M1/M6 was to be no exception.

The BMC FG series turd-brown lorry, or thrupenny bit, as they were called after the old octagonal coin, was not made for speed, but rather transporting GPO workers between their long tea breaks. The 3.8 litre diesel with its old, A road 4-speed gear box trundled laboriously north.

At the A500 crossroads to Liverpool and Manchester I spotted a lone motorcyclist, or 'greaser' walking up the slip road with motorcycle helmet in his hand. My impulse was to stop and shout him over but I figured he must be going to the big 'L' or 'M', so I left it, and droned on into the night. I realised it was the 24th November. My 28th birthday was going to happen somewhere in the middle of nowhere. That Sagittarian with Sagittarius rising thing was going to happen again, the Fool heading for the horizon with a knapsack on his back, one foot poised over the cliff's edge, eyes and heart intent on the promise of distance and greener grass on the other side of the hill. The knapsack was a truck full of clobber, wood, cupboards, a kitchen sink, a crude bed platform, an uninstalled wood burning stove.

Twenty-odd miles further on I was surprised by the flashing blue lights of a Police Range Rover. The road was empty of traffic, so I suppose a 47mph brown turd of a truck stood out like a sore thumb.

"Problem, officer?"

"Yes, you've got a back light out." I went for a look and so it was.

"I've got some light bulbs." – It was the only thing Billy Miller had ever given me, a box of bulbs and an old AA map book, the left-overs from his twenty years of driving all over the UK for Pickford's. The policeman was amazed, and held his torch while I switched bulbs.

"I was going to book you, son but I won't. It's pretty rare to find someone carrying spare bulbs."

I went to start the truck, but the battery had flaked out with leaving the lights on. The friendly policeman pushed but no go. He went and got a tow rope from his Rover and gave me a tug.

Grinding the crash box gears up the hills of the Lake District, I decided to pull in at Shap Fell services, the old resting place for horse-drawn carriages, trucks and assorted conveyances down the ages, the last big stop before the Scottish borders. By then, in 1974, it had been widened, modernised and 'Esso'-ified into a lookalike motorway service station. I filled up and while Simba went to cock a discreet leg and have a mooch, I went to pay and spotted the same greaser I had seen walking up the A500 stood by the shop entrance wearing cut-off denim jacket with Hell's Angels colours over a motorcycle leather.

"Where are you going?" I asked.

"Glasgow" – in a thick Scottish accent.

"I'm going on the high road to Edinburgh."

"Thanks, that'll be bonny."

Jamie was a cool and lucid guy. He had been visting friends in Birmingham when his bike blew up. He told me an amazing story as we branched off the old high road, the A49 via Teviothead to Edinburgh.

Him and his Hell's Angel mates used to run a youth club in Glasgow. They started getting too much pressure from the Police so him and a pal got on their bikes and rode south to the Lake District to chill out. One morning, checking over their bikes outside a greasy spoon café, an old boy approached them.

"D'you want to buy an old motor bike?"

"Why not? We'll come for a look.."

He took them to a shed behind his house and showed them a motor bike trussed up in an old oil-soaked tarpaulin. It was a Vincent Black Shadow bought new by the old boy twenty years before. He had only used it a couple of times before having a minor prang which had nevertheless left him with a broken leg. His friends had rescued the bike and wrapped it up in the proverbial oily rag. Jamie bought it for £50.

The bent forks were soon straightened, the machine overhauled and returned to original condition. Jamie became a street prince of the bikers on one of the last of the great all-English motor bikes. The Scottish Transport Museum offered him £1,000 – no way. £2,000 – no way. Later, visiting London, their Transport Museum offered him £3,000 – he took it. Some of the cash he invested, the rest he splashed out on a continental journey. Him and his mate got the job of road-testing the new Laverda for his mates Dad's shop.

They stopped over at the Hilton Hotel in Park Lane, dressed in their Hells Angels Colours. On the way back from Europe they stuffed their M/C leathers and panniers with contraband fags and booze. Looking like two puffed-up Michelin men they headed for the new hovercraft ferry to Ramsgate.

"When was that?" I said, in a flash of memory.

"July 24th." – it was the same two Michelin men motorcyclists I had spotted as we were getting (non-) busted with our American cop pal. Right instinct, Mrs VAT Woman, but wrong people!

As we waggled our way up the curvy border roads a hedgehog suddenly appeared in our headlights and scuttled out of the way. I thought nothing of it. Jamie looked at me.

"D'ye ken the hedeghog's undergone a major evolutionary change?"

"What?" I said, trying to digest his meaningful mouthful. He was dead right and the hedgehog was alive. Our textbook teachers had always told us that the spiky hedgehog rolled up into a ball to defend itself. This one had definitely run for it – I know it's true because I saw another one run just recently. I walked into my brother-in-law Simon's living room late one evening. The garden doors are often open to our wild meadow garden and there are a couple of cool, damp stone-built store rooms under the pavement. A hedgehog scuttled across my path, maybe a foot away. The surprising thing was that it had quite long furry legs and it really shifted, poor thing – mustn't let on to the authorities or we'll be getting taxed or attacked by the animal rights posse.

So much for the 'thick' image of the Hell's Angels.

The cusp of my 28th birthday passed around the Border. I'd made it! So many famous and not-so-famous people in my generation had died in their 27th year, Janice Joplin, Jimi Hendrix, Brian Jones, mostly of class A drug abuse and occupying their own fantasies courtesy of Rock'n'Roll royalties. I had also escaped from London. That choice of going straight or being part of a scene which would succumb to white powder and pills with a clutch of deaths and ruined lives.

I was on the road to nowhere and am writing this on the road to somewhere in Southern Spain; a space I am occupying 30 years later for better or worse and despite being a sometimes, schoolteacher, home-owner, husband and parent of two young people now in their twenties.

We camped overnight near Edinburgh and Jamie left en route home to Glasgow. Having escaped London, survived to 28, travelled with an enlightened soul who I had 'met' on the road and crossed the border, I felt a sense of renewal and heading in the right direction, albeit north in wintertime! I checked the pretty city and motored on to Aberdeen and the Rudolph Steiner school at Camp Hill.

The school's intake was kids with what we would call "learning difficulties". The Norwegian wood campus boasted a neat array of funky but functional two-tone buildings. There were quite a few wise old German couples about and some younger volunteers. The organisation was strict and different to my laid-back, laissez-faire existence: proper meal times and sit-down food, open, honest discussion and lots of work going on around the grounds.

I was skint as usual and had to earn my keep. I got given a job felling 4-5 clusters of twenty year-old ash regrowth. Basically the wood had been felled of big trees twenty years before. Four to five saplings had grown strong and straight out of each root. I had to take three to four and leave the strongest to grow unimpeded by its sapling brothers and sisters.

It was moving work, literally on the edge of a steep hillside. I whittled my way through it in a couple of days while Simba chased wildfowl about the flood plain below.

The strict regime and ordered activities of the school intimidated me, mostly because I suddenly felt useless and out on a limb with my truckload of junk salvaged from skips. My sense of freedom was being replaced by loneliness. I hitch-hiked "home" to London for Christmas, getting stuck on motorway junctions with a frightened Simba; got a Christmas Eve lift with a completely drunk lorry driver on a, luckily, deserted motorway. I whacked him several times to stop him driving into bridge supports.

Christmas was the usual sad, dismal, drunken affair. Billy Miller didn't know how to do anything other than drink when he wasn't working. You could set the clock by him leaving at 12 on Sundays for the boozer in cavalry twill blazer with regimental badge and matching tie. It had been the same throughout my adolescence, sitting in horrible Holloway Road boozers, being force-fed pints while my Mum graduated from Guiness to gin.

Back at home I would end up as referee as these two sad souls flung insults and plates of dinner across the room. Christmas was no exception. In fact, it was worse because there was more drinking time. Billy Miller hated any unnecessary luxuries or comfort. He was tight, organised and mean. My Mum, on the other hand was creative, erratic and generous. She always bought enough food to feed her flown daughters and dead sons.

I would have to eat three dinners, one for me two for my dead brothers which was difficult, on the one hand because I was still a semi-vegetarian, easy on the other because I'm a six foot tall, hollow-legged glutton. The drunken aggression combined with the dark depression of winter and the sadness of dead and lost siblings always made it the unhappiest day of the year for me. My children would later suffer my anti-Christmas attitude, disguised as anti-consumerist rhetoric.

With no particular place to go and nothing much to do, I was beginning to suffer from the 'unbearable lightness of being'. My handful of friends had dispersed to parents and I didn't want to return to No. 9, Clissold Road.

A part of me relished this scenario. It cut deep beneath the human veneer of comfort and companionship. I regarded certain friendships as curtain to pull over the vast expanse of solitude, a kind of cop-out. I thought of red woman on the wall girl and her low-key, non-consumerist outlook and rang her in a chance moment. She was on her way back to London and we agreed to meet.

Despite my intellectual reluctance to lean on another with my fundamental loneliness, I found that we got along really well and suggested she join me in Scotland.

We travelled by train and collected the truck from Aberdeen. We motored up hill and down dale to Martin Turner's mother's old house in a place called Camusbain at the end of a very long Loch south of Poolewe in Wester Ross. The scenery was stunning in that green grass, brown bracken, purple heather, rolling rock horizon, raging sky sort of way that typifies Scottish topography. My own soul ached for a faraway cabin in the wood up the hill, a home I could call my own away from modern mayhem and fractured family past. The problem was that there was no capital or capacity for earning it, only a big pair of hands. Next door, there was another old abandoned croft, a robust building in need of a good clean, some glass in the windows and a couple of doors, but otherwise intact.

We decided to squat this lovely building on the Saturday. The Sunday we set to sweeping and shovelling away generations of sheep shit to expose a colourful Victorian tiled floor. I went outside with a bucket of rubbish to find two policemen standing on rocks, one behind, one in front. It felt like an ambush. I dropped my bucket and put my hands up.

"Looks like you've got me surrounded, boys!"

"What are ye doing in the hoose?"

"We're squatting it."

"No ye're not. Maybe ye've no heerd of the Trespass (Scotland) Act?"

Of course, I hadn't, but it figured. If you stole somebody's country off them and they didn't like you, there would be pretty draconian laws to stop them stealing it back, particularly if you were an absentee landlord. How had they found us, 16 miles up a peninsula with precious few houses? The answer was simple. Across the loch, barely distinguishable, was a small naval station with world-wide surveillance equipment. We were right under their noses.

One day I was weaving back along the track-cum-road and my back wheels dropped into the ditch. I tried too frantically to get them out and broke a half-shaft. In those days it sounded incredibly complicated. In fact it's only the shaft that converts the wheel to the back axle and a one hour job if you've got the parts.

We went into the nearest ten-house village with a garage. The two mechanics came out to look, told me the problem. I asked them if they wanted to buy it.

"Sixty quid." That sounded OK because I'd only paid £65 for it. We dumped all the stuff in Martin's garage and hitch-hiked south. Luckily, we had met a team of university divers who were willing to give us a lift to Fort William where we knew some people.

We had to wait for them at a single house at a ferry crossing on a loch while they went diving. The house doubled up as a post office and bed and breakfast. We knocked up the owner, a cheerful lady in her 60s, asking for a drink. She made us a gigantic fisherman's fry-up breakfast that even I found difficult to finish.

We stayed with some pals of pals in Fort William. He was a dope-smoking Londoner who had got himself transferred to being the guard on the Fort William train, on the same salary plus a free house; good move.

Sandra, a friend from London was visiting that night. I slept sound and dreamt of meeting a rabbit. The next morning we went out for a hike in the heather and found a half blind, immobilised rabbit with mixamatosis.

We headed south to London again. It was time for me to find some work and buy a new truck.

THE ROAD TO ENLIGHTENMENT

I wasn't getting much closer to my goal of getting to India but I was beginning to practise the art of non-attachment – I had given up on my pad and dopers' community in London and headed to the unknown in Europe and the UK. I had already got myself a dog and was starting to get sidetracked by love. I was only human! I had better keep my eye on the ball. I didn't want to end up like my two American pals stuck in an Amsterdam, fairy-tale, fantasy time-warp.

Over the next three years I would carry on living this Yin/Yang, two-tone home lifestyle, always returning to the anonymous anarchic streets of London, interspersed with trucking trips to Ireland, Holland, France, Spain, and getting into emotional tangles. The trip to India would happen through a series of Karmic coincidences. Events of love, life, death, birth celebration and incarceration would occur and I would be witness to and sometimes participant in socio-cultural, political events that directly effect our lives 25 years on and I would be lucky enough to see some of the worlds most spectacular places and meet a thousand and one friendly foreign faces.

*   *   *

As with a lot of manoevres in my kink of a life I have slightly bent my own writing rules. Knowing that there are millions of us who could write a book about our lives, I had decided to avoid reminiscences and stick to the point of providing a window on the world that I have been lucky enough to pass through in the past 50 plus years as a kind of social commentary on our time.

The aim was to present 50 loosely connected anecdotes, mini adventures and mishaps in more or less chronological order that would yo-yo through time and space and throw a spotlight on our changing times and in particular the post WW2 cultural revolution that so many of us have lived through.

So much crap has been written, particularly by overpaid pundits of the press, like David Aaronovitch for example that I thought a worm's eye view might be a refreshing change.

Chapter headings like *Twin Coronation 1952, Stratford Tragedy*

1960, Paris 1968, Hitler dead? 1975, were meant to be stand alone, airport, stuck-on-a-broken-down train, waiting in casualty, short attention span mini-reads.

The next volume, the ensuing 25 plus years will stick to the plot; not least because they were more of a blur and a whirl. Chapter titles will include *Passage to India, Backwards in Afghanistan, The Buddha's False Tooth, Amsterdam Capers, Crisis Chris McAllister, Banged Up in Bulgaria, Bristol City, No Tax for Thatcher, Spanish Sierra, Goodmoves (UK and Europe), Glastonbury Mud Warriors, Montpelier Mafia, Danish Freeschools and Unradical Politicians, Dead Mothers and Brothers Rites of Passage, Rungless Property Ladders in Minimum Wage Britain, Rumanian Rescue, Teaching in the Grey Zone, Alternative Technologies and Half Baked Ideologies, Bianca Jagger's Coffee - Hyde Park 15th February, 2003.*

Paul Goodchild, Montpelier, Bristol, October 2005